Introducing
Albion Stitch

20 BEADED JEWELRY PROJECTS

Heather Kingsley-Heath

Kalmbach Books

WAUKESHA, WI

Kalmbach Books
21027 Crossroads Circle
Waukesha, Wisconsin 53186
www.JewelryandBeadingStore.com

Published in 2015
20 19 18 17 16   1 2 3 4 5

Manufactured in China

ISBN: 978-1-62700-138-0
EISBN: 978-1-62700-139-7

Editor: Karin Van Voorhees
Book Design: Lisa Bergman
Photographer: William Zuback

Library of Congress Control Number: 2015930769

Contents

Heather Kingsley Heath has contributed her solid design sense to the bead world with a body of work which ranges from sophisticated to whimsical. Heather has a large repertoire of stitches at her command, which she has used to bring us intricate designs in both sculpture and jewelry.

As the author of *Beaded Opulence, Techniques in Right Angle Weave*, I love a book that gives us a comprehensive set of skills within one beadweaving stitch. Heather has done that here, building upon the readers understanding of the stitch one chapter at a time.

In *Introducing Albion Stitch*, Heather focuses on the Albion stitch that she developed, showing us how to use it to create beautiful, feminine, and wearable jewelry.

As the chapters unfold, the reader is first introduced to the basic Albion stitch using its versatility to create bands of color and texture. Each of the five designs in Chapter 1 expands the knowledge of Albion stitch, leading one through the skills of changing stitch lengths, creating shape, and incorporating some two-hole bead shapes. Each chapter also has a color theme, encouraging beaders to explore and expand their own color selections. In Chapter 1, the retro-coastal theme of sea green, turquoise, and coral evokes the feel of a tropical ocean vacation.

In Chapter 2, the reader is invited to add even more shape while creating beaded beads, tubular ropes, and bezels. Here, the cool market garden colors of lavender, lemon, lime, and ginger with accents of primrose and violet keep our visual interest.

Chapter 3 introduces us to some delightfully feminine jewelry with the look of lace. The use of Rizo beads at the tips of the Albion stitch create medallions that are connected in varying ways to give us a variety of different looks. Heather introduces us to the idea of playing with design variations by changing the number of repetitions for a different look. The matte pastels used in this chapter add to the feeling of romance these pieces impart.

In Chapter 4, we learn how to add structure to the Albion stitch in order to create simple shaping. Here, the modestly monochrome metallic helps to highlight the structural quality of each of the pieces presented.

Each of the 20 projects presented in this book is designed not only to advance the reader's knowledge of Albion stitch, but to result in a piece of beautiful jewelry that you will be proud to wear. While the designs are ultimately very achievable, the learning, which builds from basic through advanced techniques, will result in a comprehensive understanding of this versatile stitch.

Heather has designed her projects to allow for the changing out of bead sizes and counts, allowing the reader to take the skills learned and to use the thread paths to experiment beyond the projects that are presented. She has given us a comprehensive guide to using Albion stitch and invited us to explore further.

I invite you to enjoy making the pieces presented here and continue on your own journey of exploration using Albion stitch.

Marcia DeCoster
MadDesigns
Beadweaver, Teacher, Author
Lemon Grove, Ca

Introduction

My name is Heather, and I live and work in England. I live in the West country, where I am surrounded by fields and woods, farmland and villages. I have a garden which is slightly bigger than I can manage and it is full of wildlife. Home is where I bead and make kits and patterns. On sunny days you will find me in the garden beading instead of weeding. On rainy days, which we get plenty of in England, I'll be working on the computer or sitting quietly beading, but wherever I am, there is usually a cat curled up beside me, or busy trying to "help."

Throughout the year, I travel to meet beaders and teach, both in the U. K. and overseas. I teach in stores, to groups that meet in halls, and in homes. I also attend as many bead shows as I can. There is no escaping the fact that I love beads and the beading life.

It started when I took a class and tried peyote stitch with Delica beads. Instantly hooked is the only way to describe my addiction to the tiny glass sparkles and the ingenious ways to slot them together on a strand of thread. I tried more and more techniques, and as my confidence and understanding grew, I began to make up my own designs.

I so loved this craft that I wanted to share my enthusiasm and I began to teach in a local store. Next, I used my experience as an editor to write projects for magazines and to write and publish books. Now, I sell my own patterns and kits. Each one begins as an idea I really want to explore and to wear myself. If enough people like it, too, it becomes a workshop. When the design is retired from the classroom, it becomes a pattern for sale.

ABOUT ALBION STITCH

Albion stitch began during a conversation between bead artist friends about how to bring fresh ideas into our beadwork. Sometimes just one little comment can change a life, and that is how, over tea and biscuits, an inkling of an idea grew to become several years of creative exploration.

The "little idea" tickling away, was a row of beading within a freeform brick stitch piece, where I had worked elongated picot stitches to make the piece grow more quickly.

I showed my first experiments at the next meeting. The idea was discussed, and the consensus was that I should go back to the beads and just do more.

There followed many months of test pieces, some of which grew to become the starting points for designs. Others were ripped out and re-worked, with one piece taking a record 35 rip-outs before the step in the technique was sorted. Slowly a process emerged—ways of increasing and decreasing, of getting the stitch to describe shapes and patterns. At this point, I went right back to the beginning and created a language for the stitch. I simplified the process and the steps to make it perform all the basics that any other beading stitch is able and expected to do.

With terminology in place, and flat, flat round, tubular, geometric, and dimensional forms able to be shown and described, it was time to share the stitch. My beading group tried the basic steps and loved the class. With the first trial completed, it was back to the beads again, this time to create a sequential collection of designs, each showing a new step in the process, which became the patterns in my first Albion stitch digital book. The second half of the process was revealed in my second digital book, where I shared the techniques for creating bezels, crisp geometric shapes, layered forms, and patterns for flowers, insects, and leaves.

I have taught Albion stitch in several countries. What excites me the most is that, because it is easy to learn, beaders are soon reaching for more beads to play with. It is deeply rewarding to watch everyone start the "what if" game, just having fun experimenting with beads.

In this book are designs to introduce you some of the different ways of working with Albion stitch. All the projects are designs I love to make and wear. Albion stitch is very versatile. In this book, it is used to create pretty and wearable jewelry, all designed in a way to enable you to start playing your own "what if" game, then take your own bead selections to make simple changes to the designs.

Beadwork is a gentle hobby; it requires time, a little patience, and the willingness to let a day or an afternoon slip by as you work. For me there is nothing so lovely as the calm that settles when all I have in front of me is a day of creating and a new design to play with. I hope you will enjoy exploring Albion stitch as much as I have in developing it for you.

Fundamentals

Color

A typical question in class is the one about how to choose colors. For many, it can be daunting and the more you try to work it out, the more confusing all the information can be. This is because most color theory is all about mixing paints, but with beads, we have a fixed palette—the colors the manufacturers make for us. Paints give a flat matte surface, where as our beads can be matte, shiny, opaque, or transparent. Plus, they can have a variety of finishes over the surface. So, unlike the painters, we have the additional luxury of considering how light plays across and through our beads.

At the start of each chapter, there is a color palette of inspiration images with a description of the colors used and suggestions for accent colors. The projects for the section are shown worked in the colors from the palette. The designs will work in any colors, or you can borrow color ideas from another section if you prefer them. It is just a useful tool to use if you want to.

Color inspiration is everywhere. Ready-made mixes in beautiful woven or printed textiles are a great starting point. I also take photos of things that catch my attention, because once you start looking, there are wonderful color mixes just waiting to be noticed.

In the materials lists for the projects, there are no number codes listed. Instead, a description of the bead color is given. This is because I want you to pick out your own mixes, and hopefully the color sections will inspire you to have a go. (If you want to reproduce the designs exactly, then the photographs will help you match beads at the store.)

Seed Beads

Seed beads are the heart of beadwork and the projects in this book use three different sizes of seed bead. The smallest is a 15º, this size can be used to make a whole piece, but is usually used to add accents, develop more fine detail, or to help shape a piece by dropping down in scale.

A size 10 beading needle will fit through 15º seed beads, but using a size 11 or 12 needle will be useful if you need to make more than one pass with the thread through a bead.

11º seed beads are the most commonly used bead size, and are bigger than the 15º. A size 10 beading nee-dle is the right size for the beads and the beads will easily take several passes of beading thread.

8º seed beads are bigger again! The larger the seed bead, the lower the size number. 8º seed beads are great for making larger scale jewelry, and for practicing with. They are also used as accent beads and to help shape a piece by scaling up in bead size.

Bead brands

Most of my samples are worked in Miyuki seed beads, simply because here in my corner of England, they are easily available. If you are new to beading you may not recognize manufacturers' names. A 11º round seed bead made by one manufacturer can be slightly different in the shape and overall size to one made by another manufacturer.

For many designs, this matters not one bit, but for designs which need a precise fit (for example a bezel for a cabochon), it can make a big difference. For those designs where it will make a difference, Miyuki will be listed at the top of the materials list.

Good bead stores will always tell you which brands they carry—Miyuki, Toho, Matsuno or Czech seed beads. As your experience grows, you will be able to tell the differences between bead brands and recognize when it is important to use the brand if a designer has specified one for their project in books or magazines.

Bead Types

In the last few years, new beads have come thick and fast. The first two-hole beads had us all excited, and now you can buy two-hole beads in all sorts of shapes. Designers have started working with manufacturers to bring us even more variations to play with: four-hole beads, beads with oval holes, even more shape variety, too. I've incorporated new beads wherever possible in the designs. The shapes and sizes of beads used in this book are pictured on p. 9.

Cabochons

We beaders love to incorporate other elements into our beadwork, and one of the easiest ways is to bead a bezel to hold a cabochon. I've used LunaSoft flat back cabochons and Swarovski 14mm Rivoli. The Rivoli have pointed backs.

Clasps and Closures

If I'm making a special commission or exhibition piece, I will always make a beaded clasp—but for every-day jewelry, I prefer to use store-bought clasps. They do the job, will take lots of wear, and come in such a variety that you can easily find one to match the style of the beaded piece. I use sliding clasps with loops for wider bracelets and cuffs, lobster clasps and jump rings for necklaces, and snap fasteners for hidden clasps. Like all craft materials, it pays to invest in the best quality findings and to shop around for a supplier who carries a range that appeals to you.

Bead Types

Seed beads (15°, 11°, 8°)

3mm bugle beads

Czech fire polished 3mm
and 5mm

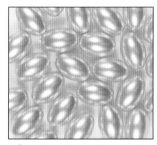

Czech 6x4mm rice pearls

Czech two-hole
6mm Pyramid beads

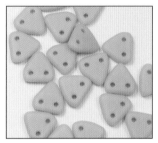

CzechMate two-hole
6mm triangles

CzechMate two-hole
3x6mm bricks

CzechMate two-hole
6mm tiles

CzechMate two-hole
6mm lentils

Miyuki Magatama 4x7mm

Miyuki 1.8mm cube beads

Pellet or Diablo
4x6mm beads

SuperDuo 2.5x5mm
two-hole beads

Swarovski
4mm bicone crystals

Swarovski
4mm rose montees

Cords, Ribbons, and Chains

Combining beadwork with other materials is fun. I like this mixed-media look for some pieces, and so for some designs in the book, I've used silk ribbons and hand-made ribbon made from T-shirt material. Like bead variety, the number and styles of chain we can buy by the yard has grown hugely. I've used hollow mesh chain which is very slinky, and, with care, you can stitch beaded bails to the ends. This is a nice way to bring beadwork and metal chains and clasps together at the back of the necklace.

Needles and Thread

Our choice for threads and needles just keeps on growing. I use K.O. beading thread and FireLine 6 lb. test braided thread. There are lots of thread brands to choose from, and I recommend that you try as many as possible, then choose which feels right for you. As your experience grows, you'll find each thread has its uses and you'll have a stash of your favorites to select from.

Thread is available in lots of colors so you can match them to your beads. Over the years, I've found that a light beige, ash, or sand color will work with most beads, as the thread "disappears" into the shadows. It is worth taking the time to work a little sample using the same beads but with different thread colors to see what happens.

Then, continue with the thread color that creates the effect you like best.

Needles for beading are fine, with a straight eye. They come in a range of sizes. Size 10 is a medium thickness and fine for all the projects in this book. It's useful to have a finer needle, an 11 or 12, in your bead box as sometimes a bead can get filled with thread. Dropping down a needle size can help ease a thread through. Beading needles are widely available in two lengths: long (5cm) or short (3cm). Try both and see which suits you best. If you prefer the longer ones, just keep a short one on hand, as it is useful for weaving thread tails back into the beadwork.

If you find that your thread is fraying, change your needle for a new one. Needle eyes are punched out on a machine, then polished, but sometimes a minuscule burr of metal can remain hidden in the eye.

If you find it hard to thread a beading needle (even with your reading glasses on), try turning the needle around to come at the eye from the other side; that punching process that creates the needle eye means that one side of the eye has a slightly different edge than the other.

All the Other Things

With a **comfortable place to sit and bead**, it is easy to get lost in the beads and have several hours go by. Make sure that you are not straining your neck, shoulders or back. Having room to spread out is also a good idea, as you will need space for a bead mat, book, boxes of beads, and a mug of something nice to drink. As your love of this craft grows, so will your stash of useful things to help you.

Have a pair of small, sharp **embroidery scissors** and dedicate them to only your bead thread.

A **bead mat** is your workstation, so invest in the best you can. You can buy bead mat fabric and lay it in a tray, or clip it into a flat picture frame, or treat yourself to a beautiful handmade board. I find that a neutral color, like cream or ivory, works best for me.

Choose a **craft lamp** fitted with a good quality daylight bulb, because your eyes deserve the best, too.

I also have a **clip-on reading light** with daylight bulbs, which uses rechargeable batteries. It's a great additional light source in the evenings, and ideal when traveling.

A fine **awl** or small **needlenose pliers** are useful. If you find you need to pop out a bead, the awl can be pushed into the bead hole until the bead pops. If you prefer pliers, always slide your needle into the rogue bead first,

then crack the bead with the pliers. Having the needle in place will protect the thread from accidental cutting by any sharp edges of the broken bead.

Little **scoops** make light work of tidying away the beads.

A **note pad and pencil** are handy to make notes of the bead colors you've used, or notes-to-self to remember any changes you make to a design, such as length.

If you're new to beading and not sure about supplies, find your nearest bead store and make yourself known. The beading community is very welcoming and many stores also host beading groups and classes. If you are a long way from a bead store, our community can come to you via the internet—stores offer online shopping therapy and Facebook is full of friendly beading groups and links to designers' blogs and home pages.

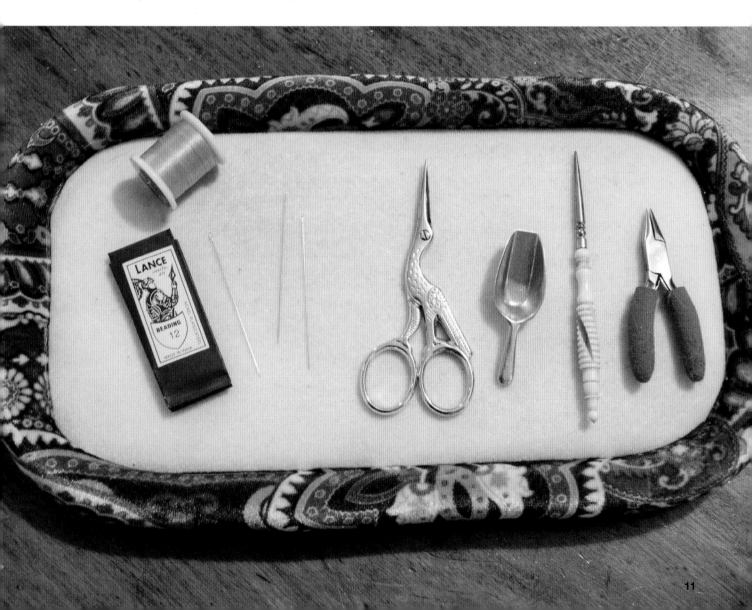

fig. 1

fig. 2

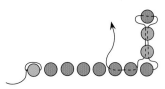

fig. 3

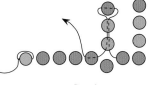

fig. 4

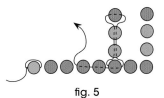

fig. 5

Introduction to Albion Stitch

If you are familiar with beadwork techniques, you will recognize the elements of Albion stitch: First you will create picots, which are then strung together through the tips, with the option of adding a single peyote-stitch row to create different effects.

As I developed the stitch and began to teach it, I found that a set of simple terms to describe the stitch with its own language was more useful than the brief description above. I use these terms throughout the book to make the instructions for variations and patterns easy to follow. Refer back to these pages if you need to check the basics as you work.

Foundation Row or Base Row

This is a row of beads with an even or odd number. For flat techniques, use a stop bead and then remove it once the first row of stitches is completed **(fig. 1)**. A stop bead is a spare bead attached to the thread in a way that it can be removed easily. It is simply there to stop all the other beads from falling off the thread while you begin to bead.

A Ring of Beads

Tubular techniques are worked from a foundation ring made from an even number of beads **(fig. 2)**.

The Stitch: Stalk and Tip

One or more beads form the stalk and one or more beads form the tip. To make the stitch, pick up the stalk and tip beads together, then pass back down through the stalk beads. The tip bead will flip over and lie at a right angle to the stalk bead(s) when the thread is tightened.

"Stitch Above" the Foundation Bead

To "stitch above," bring the needle out of the end foundation bead. Pick up beads for the stalk and tip, pass back through the stalk, and pass through the second foundation bead.

The stitch will sit above the end foundation bead **(fig. 3)**. This is how each row starts for flat Albion stitch.

Stitches worked above beads within the foundation row using this method will cause the foundation row beads to move out of alignment **(fig. 4)**.

"Stitch Over" the Foundation Bead

The placement of the stitch (stalk and tip) is an essential move to keep the foundation row straight and smooth.

To "stitch over," bring the needle through the foundation bead, left to right (or vice versa), pick up the stalk and tip beads, pass back through the stalk, and back through the foundation bead from left to right again (or vice versa) **(fig. 5)**.

This will anchor the stitch over the foundation bead. Always exit the foundation row bead that you want the stitch to sit over, and re-enter it once the stitch is made.

For **tubular Albion stitch**, all the stitches are worked in the same way to sit over the foundation ring bead **(fig. 6)**.

How to End a Row and Step Up
Work the last stitch **(fig. 7)** and then remove the stop bead. Tie the working thread to the tail, and pass back through the stalk and tip beads of the last stitch **(fig. 8)**.

Spacer Row
After you have stepped up through the last stalk and tip worked, you are in position to make the spacer row.

Pick up a single bead then pass through the next tip bead. Repeat to the end of the row **(fig. 9)**. The tip and spacer beads now form the base or new foundation row for the next row of Albion stitch.

The spacer row can be used to increase, and so you might be asked to pick up two or more spacer beads between each tip.

The spacer row can be used to decrease, in which case you might be asked to pass through tip beads without adding spacer beads between them.

Another Form of Foundation Row
Peyote stitch can create an edge, which makes it easy to add Albion stitches above a bead. **(fig. 10)** effectively illustrates adding an Albion stitch between the raised peyote beads. This can be worked as a flat or tubular foundation.

Terminology and Pattern Style
The materials list at the beginning of each project shows the bead quantity, size, and type. Each bead is given a letter. In the instructions, the letter will be used to tell you which beads to pick up:

So if the first bead to use is an 11° seed bead (A), the instructions will show: pick up 12xA, so you pick up 12 11° seed beads.

If a design uses more than one color of the same size bead, the materials list will show a letter for each color: 10g 11° seed beads each in three colors, A, B, C.

A thread tail is left at the start and end of each thread. Always have a tail 10–15cm (4–6 in.); it should be long enough to thread a needle on so you can weave the tail back into the beadwork.

How much thread? Use a single thickness of thread. We beaders like to use a longer thread than our sewing sisters. Don't try to use more than an arm span (one meter). All you will do is wear out your arms, the thread, and your patience as you untangle.

Starting a New Thread
Some designers will advocate never knotting the thread; others, myself included, are happy to use knots. I have a really quick and easy one. It can be used to start a new thread partway through a piece or to start a ring of

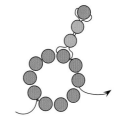

fig. 6

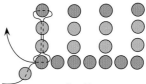

fig. 7

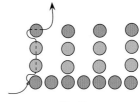

fig. 8

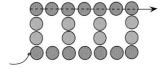

fig. 9

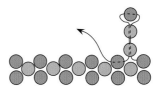

fig. 10

beads if a pattern calls for one.

Take the needle off the old tail. Cut a new length of thread. Bring one end of the new thread side-by-side to the tail **(fig. 11** and **fig. 12)**.

Make a loop of both threads together **(fig. 13)**.

Pass the short ends through the loop **(fig. 14)**.

Gently tighten the knot so it is near the beadwork. Now take the old and new tails, one in each hand and pull them apart until the knot slides down to the last bead used **(fig. 15)**.

Now you can carry on beading for a bit, then go back later to finish off the thread tails **(fig. 16)**.

Making a Loop of Beads

Thread the beads on and leave a 6-in. (15cm) tail. Now make the same knot, but instead of putting the tails through the loop, pop the "noose" of beads through the loop, and then pull the two threads until the knot slides down to the beads **(fig. 17)**.

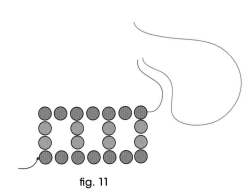

fig. 11

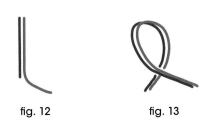

fig. 12   fig. 13

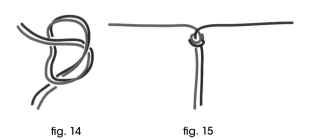

fig. 14   fig. 15

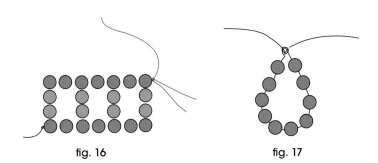

fig. 16   fig. 17

Flat Albion Stitch

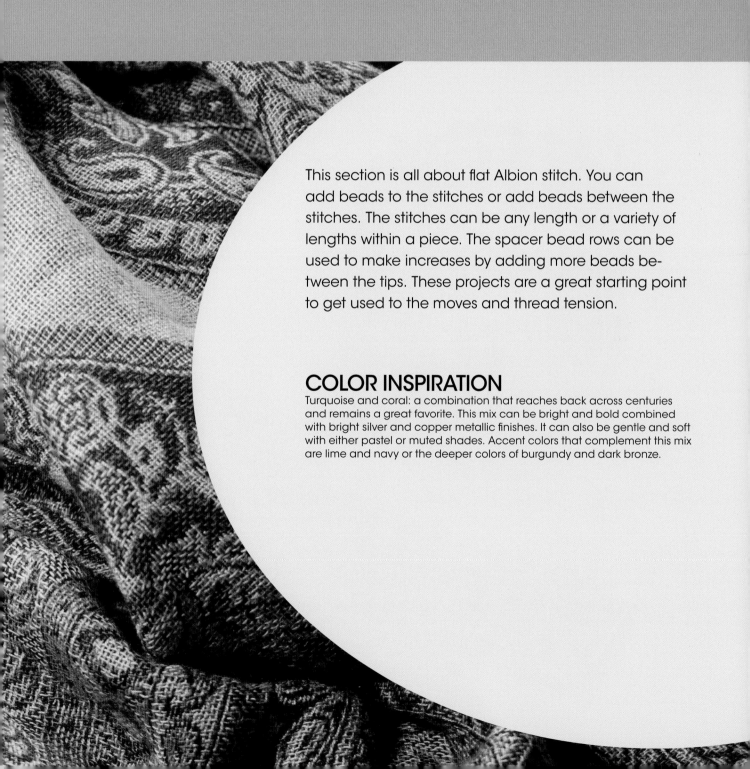

This section is all about flat Albion stitch. You can add beads to the stitches or add beads between the stitches. The stitches can be any length or a variety of lengths within a piece. The spacer bead rows can be used to make increases by adding more beads between the tips. These projects are a great starting point to get used to the moves and thread tension.

COLOR INSPIRATION

Turquoise and coral: a combination that reaches back across centuries and remains a great favorite. This mix can be bright and bold combined with bright silver and copper metallic finishes. It can also be gentle and soft with either pastel or muted shades. Accent colors that complement this mix are lime and navy or the deeper colors of burgundy and dark bronze.

These flat bands are worked in matte finish beads. Although simple, a scattering of crystals and metallic beads adds a gentle sparkle. The stitches are placed over the beads of the base row, and the first stitch is worked in a slightly different way to ensure it sits over the first bead of the base row.

Sparkle Bands

materials

8⁰ seed beads

A 10g matte red AB

B 10g metallic pewter

C 10g matte frosted orange AB

D 36 3mm bicone or fire-polished beads, astral pink AB

E 5g 11⁰ seed beads, metallic pewter

- 3-strand sliding clasp or similar, copper

The bracelet shown measures 17cm (7 in.), not including clasp. Each arch uses 7xD. Each arch section measures 1cm (½ in.), including the embellished row.

Stitch the Band

1 Secure a stop bead. Pick up alternating A and B beads, starting with A and ending with A, until you have a total of 11 beads. Push them down to the stop bead **(fig. 1)**.

The next step is to place stitches over each A bead of the base row (see p. 12).

2 Stitch 1: Pick up 2xC (stalk); 1xA (tip), pass back through the 2xC, and pull up the thread. Pass over the first A bead on the base row (the one the thread is coming from), and then pass through the next two beads (B, A) of the base row. Pull the thread up. The first stitch should now sit at a right angle to the base row and over the end A bead **(fig. 2)**.

3 Stitch 2: Pick up 2xC (stalk); 1xA (tip), pass back through 2xC, then pass back through the 1xA base row bead. Pass through the next two beads (B, A) of the base row to be in place to start the next stitch. Pull the thread up firmly **(fig. 3)**.

4 Repeat step 3 **(fig. 4)**.

5 Repeat step 3 two more times. The thread will come out of the end A bead of the base row after the second repeat **(fig. 5)**. Remove the stop bead and tie the tail thread to the working thread.

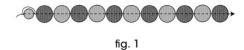

fig. 1

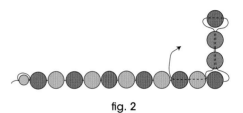

fig. 2

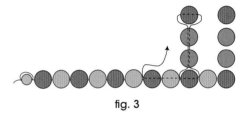

fig. 3

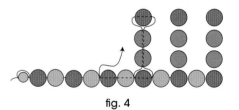

fig. 4

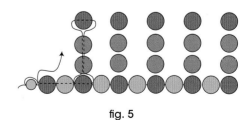

fig. 5

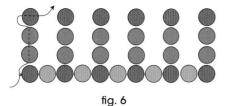

fig. 6

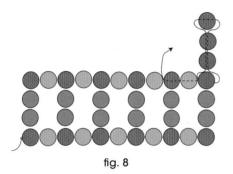

fig. 7

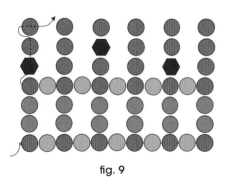

fig. 8

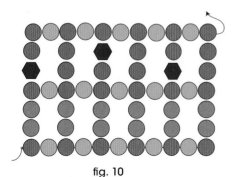

fig. 9

fig. 10

6 For the final stitch of the row, pick up 2xC (stalk); 1xA (tip), pass back through the 2xC, and pass back through the end A bead of the base row. Pull the thread up. To step up to start the next row, pass back through the stalk and tip (2xC, 1xA) of the last stitch and exit the tip bead **(fig. 6)**.

7 Spacer row (see p. 13): Pick up 1xB, pass through the next tip bead. Repeat until the thread exits the tip bead of the first stitch worked In step 1. The spacer row is now the same as the base row, and forms the base row for the next set of stitches **(fig. 7)**.

8 The next row of stitches is worked in the same way as the first row of stitches, but with different beads:

Stitches 1, 3, and 5: 2xA (stalk); 1xA (tip)
Stitches 2 and 6: 1xD, 1xA (stalk); 1xA (tip)
Stitch 4: 1xA, 1xD (stalk); 1xA (tip)
(fig. 8 and 9).

9 Step up through the last stitch, then work a spacer row of 1xB between each tip bead **(fig. 10)**.

10 Third row: Pick up 2xC (stalk); 1xA (tip). Step up through the last stitch, then work a spacer row of 1xB between each tip bead **(fig. 11)**.

11 Fourth row:

Stitches 1, 5: 1xA, 1xD (stalk); 1xA (tip)
Stitches 2, 4, and 6: 2xA (stalk); 1xA (tip)
Stitch 3: 1xD, 1xA, (stalk); 1xA (tip)
Step up through the last stitch. Work a spacer row of 1xB between each tip bead **(fig. 12)**.

12 Keep working the sequence of rows until the bracelet is the right length to fit your wrist. I worked 25 rows for a bracelet measuring 17.5cm (7 in.), not including the clasp.

Embellish the Edges

13 With the thread coming from the end bead of the last spacer row, pick up 1xE and pass through the stalk beads of the end stitch of the previous row.

14 Pick up 3xE and pass through the stalk beads of the end stitch of the previous row **(fig. 13)**.

15 Repeat step 14 to the end of the bracelet band. Pick up 1xE, pass through the base row, pick up 1xE, and pass through the stalk beads of the end stitch on the second side of the band. Pick up 3xE and pass through the stalk beads of the next end stitch **(fig. 14)**.

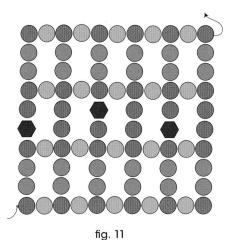

fig. 11

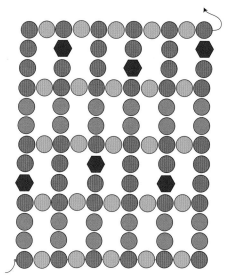

fig. 12

16 Keep working along the second side, adding 3xE between pairs of stalk beads. At the end of the row, finish with 1xE and pass through the end spacer row.

Add a Clasp

1 Use any thread tails to work back through the end rows of the beadwork to strengthen them. Use a new thread, so, if the clasp wears you can cut this thread without cutting into the threads of your beadwork.

2 Align the clasp with the end of the bracelet and bring the needle out of the bead nearest the first loop of the clasp. Pass through the loop, tuck the needle under the thread of the beadwork on the other side of the bead, and then pass back through the loop.

3 Pass back through the same bead started from, then do the loop and tuck move from step 2 a few more times. I like to roll the beadwork slightly over the loop of the clasp and tighten it into place with the thread. When the first loop is secure, move on to the next one, passing through the end row beads.

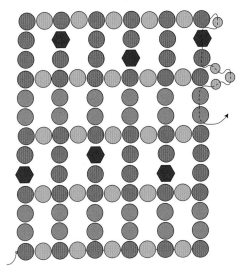

fig. 13

note

The basic band of flat Albion stitch can be worked in all sorts of bead combinations. The light green design uses the same bead sizes but the stalks are three 8° seed beads high and the rows alternate between rows of 3x8° stalk, 1x8° tip, and rows with stalks of 1x8°, 1x3mm crystal, 1x8°; and a tip of 1x8°. The edges are embellished in the same way.

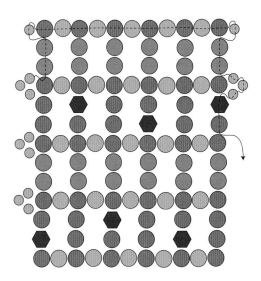

fig. 14

Fan Dance looks at a simple way of increasing, by adding stitches over every bead of the base row. Adding a spacer row makes the stitches fan out to form a new base row with twice as many beads in it. This design starts from a ring of beads, so no stop bead is needed. Fan Dance uses Czech glass beads called *pellets,* also known as *Diablo* beads. These beads have flat tops and a "waist" with a single hole through it, where the seed beads can nestle.

Fan Dance

11º seed beads
- **A** 10g matte frosted turquoise
- **B** 10g lined coral red
- **C** 10g lined coral pink

- **D** 33–42 4mm Czech glass pellet (Diablo) beads

- 2 9mm metal snap fasteners

Note on quantities: To calculate how many pellet (D) beads you will need, each segment uses 3xD and measures 1.7cm (⁵⁄₈ in.). The bracelets shown have 11 segments and measure 18cm (7 in.).

fig. 1

fig. 2

1 Pick up 12xA and secure them in a ring to form the base ring **(fig. 1)**.

2 Pick up 1xD and pass through the sixth bead from the start point **(fig. 2)**. Pass back through the 1xD. Pass through the next 3xA from the start point **(fig. 3)**.

fig. 3

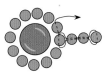

fig. 4

3 The first stitch row: Stitches are placed over seven beads of the base row. Because the beads are being worked on a ring base, all the stitches are worked in the same way.

Stitch 1: 2xA (stalk); Pick up 1xA (tip), pass back through 2xA, then pass back through the first base ring bead.

Pass through the next bead on the base ring and pull the thread up. The first stitch is in place and the thread is in place to start the next stitch **(fig. 4)**.

4 Stitch 2: Pick up 2xB (stalk); 1xA (tip) **(fig. 5)** Repeat four times.

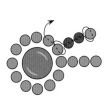

fig. 5

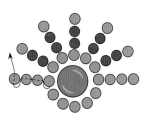

fig. 6

5 Stitch 3 (last): Pick up 2xA (stalk); 1xA (tip). Step up through the last stitch worked to exit the tip bead **(fig. 6)**.

6 Spacer Row: Pick up 1xA between each 1xA tip bead **(fig. 7)**. Now you are in place to create another row of stitches, with one stitch over each bead of the base row. (The first stitch is worked differently from the others; just as it is for a flat band.)

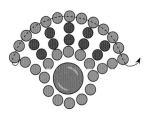

fig. 7

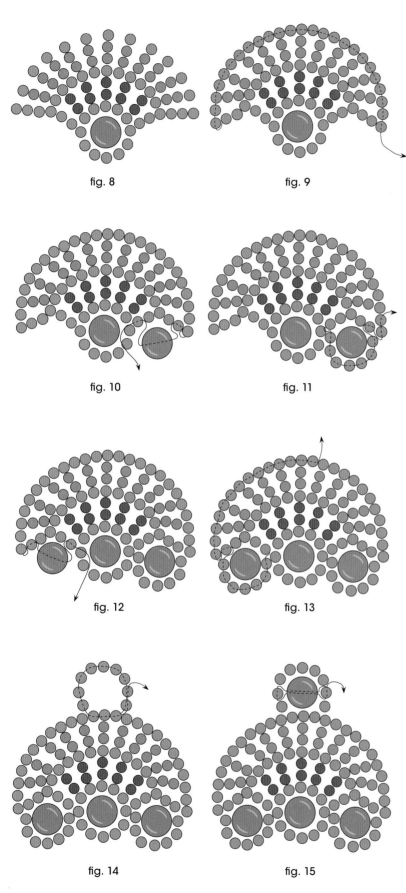

fig. 8

fig. 9

fig. 10

fig. 11

fig. 12

fig. 13

fig. 14

fig. 15

7 Stitch 1: Pick up 2xA (stalk); 1xA (tip). Pass through the second bead of the base row. Pull the thread firmly so the stitch will sit over the first bead of the base row. The thread is in place to start the next stitch.

Stitches 2–12: Pick up 2xC (stalk); 1xA (tip)
Stitch 13: 2xA (stalk); 1xA (tip) **(fig. 8)**.
Step up through the last stitch worked to exit the tip bead.

8 Spacer Row: Pick up 1xA between each 1xA tip bead **(fig. 9)**.

9 Pass back through the first stalk bead (nearest the tip bead) of the first stitch worked. Pick up 1xD. Pass through the second stalk bead (nearest base ring) and the first stitch of the first row worked. Pull the thread firmly **(fig. 10)**.

10 Pick up 7xA, pass back through the bead started from at the beginning of step 9, and pass through the tip bead of the last spacer bead of the second row **(fig. 11)**.

11 Weave through the spacer bead row to reach the other side of the beadwork. Repeat steps 9 and 10 **(fig. 12)**. Pass the needle through the spacer row to exit the 14th bead from the end of the row **(fig. 13)**.

Now you are in place to start the next segment. The new base ring will share three beads of the spacer row of the completed segment. This is how each new segment will start.

12 Pick up 9xA. Pass through the center three beads of the spacer row (beads 12, 13, 14). Then pass through the first 2xA of the 9xA just added **(fig. 14)**.

13 Pick up 1xD, and pass through the sixth bead from the start point of the ring. Pass back through the 1xD and through the bead started from **(fig. 15)**.

14 For this step, stitches are placed over seven beads of the new base ring, starting from the second of the new beads added in step 11, and ending on the second to last bead **(fig. 16)**.

Stitch 1: Pick up 2xA (stalk); 1xA (tip)
Stitches 2–6: Pick up 2xB (stalk); 1xA (tip)
Stitch 7: Pick up 2xA (stalk); 1xA (tip)
To complete the second segment, repeat steps 7–11.

Repeat to work as many segments as you need to make the bracelet the length required.

Add a Tab for the Snap Fastener Closure

1 Complete the final segment and step up through the beads as if to start a new segment.

Add 9xA to make the base ring beads, but exit the sixth bead instead of the second **(fig 17)**.

2 Pick up 3xA. Pass back through the center 3xA of the base ring (beads 4, 5, 6). Pass back through the 3xA just added **(fig. 18)**.

3 Pick up 3xA, pass back through the 3xA of step 2, then pass back through the 3xA just added **(fig. 19)**.

4 Pick up 9xA, and pass back through the 3xA added in step 3. Weave through the new ring of 12xA once more **(fig. 20)**.

Stitch the snap fasteners over the two rings of beads created in the tab. Stitch the other halves over the base ring of the first segment (and pellet bead) and over the beads above them, so the snaps on the tab line up. Stitch through the holes in the snap fasteners and between the beads of the beadwork. (See note with photo, below.)

fig. 16

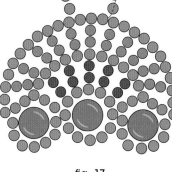

fig. 17

fig. 18

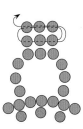

fig. 19

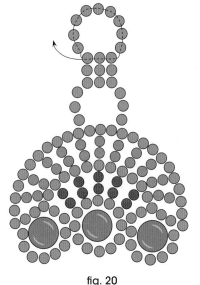

fig. 20

note

SNAP FASTENERS

First patented in 1858, snap fasteners have held clothing, bags, saddlery, and jewelry together ever since. They are a perfect solution for hidden closures. Good quality snap fasteners will hold a bracelet together; I use two in line for added security. Metal or plastic versions will both work, but don't go smaller than 9mm. The silver-edged bracelet has a half segment, which supports two snap fasteners side by side as an alternative layout.

This bracelet demonstrates how bead choices can change the shape of the beadwork to create a different kind of increase while working with regular rows. Because the bead sizes change within rows, you will need to keep a good tension on the thread.

Chic Lizard

materials

11º seed beads

A 8g metallic dark bronze

B 8g matte frosted turquoise

C 8g lined coral red

8º seed beads

D 5g metallic dark bronze

E 5g matte frosted turquoise

F 36–48 CzechMate two-hole triangle beads

• 3-strand sliding clasp or similar, antique copper

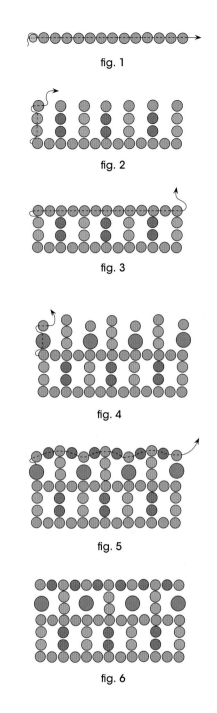

fig. 1

fig. 2

fig. 3

fig. 4

fig. 5

fig. 6

1 Secure a stop bead. Pick up 13xA and push them down to the stop bead **(fig. 1)**.

2 Stitch Row 1: The stitches of this row alternate stalk-bead colors and they sit over the first and alternate beads of the base row.
    Stitch 1: Pick up 2xB (stalk); 1xA (tip)
    Stitch 2: Pick up 2xC (stalk); 1xA (tip)
    At the end of the row, remove the stop bead, secure the tail to the working thread, then step up through the beads of the last stitch to exit the tip bead **(fig. 2)**.

3 Spacer Row: Pick up 1xA between each 1xA tip bead **(fig. 3)**.

4 Stitch Row 2: This row also has alternating stitches, but this time the beads change:
    Stitch 1: Pick up 1xD (stalk); 1xA (tip)
    Stitch 2: Pick up 2xB (stalk); 1xA (tip)
    The stitches will differ slightly in length; this is fine and will even out at the next step. At the end of the row, step up through the last stitch of the row **(fig. 4)**.

5 Spacer Row: Pick up 1xC between each 1xA tip bead **(fig. 5)**. Pull the thread firmly so the beads straighten into a neat row **(fig. 6)**.

note

THREAD TENSION

The tip bead in Albion stitch works like a locking mechanism: The thread is trapped by the sides of the tip bead, which push it against the hole of the nearest stalk bead. To release the thread and pull it up tight, hold the tip bead while pulling the thread. Once the thread is tight, release the tip bead.

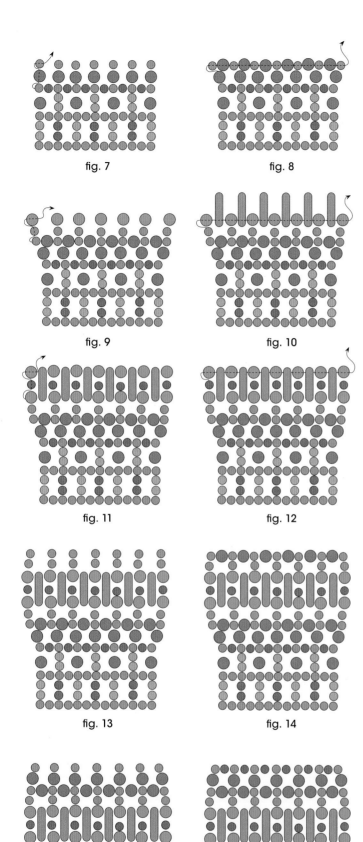

fig. 7

fig. 8

fig. 9

fig. 10

fig. 11

fig. 12

fig. 13

fig. 14

fig. 15

fig. 16

6 Stitch Row 3: The seven stitches of this row are all the same: 1xD (stalk); 1xA (tip). Step up at the end of the row **(fig. 7)**.

7 Spacer Row: Pick up 1xD between each 1xA tip bead. This widens the row and starts the increase section. The increase is made by using bigger beads; the number of beads remains the same. **(fig. 8)**.

8 Stitch Row 4: The stitches of this row are all the same, but the bead size is reversed:
　　1xA (stalk); 1xE (tip)
　　Step up through the last stitch at the end of the row **(fig. 9)**.

9 Spacer Row: This spacer row has a difference. It uses a two-hole triangle bead as the spacer bead. Only one hole of the bead is passed through and you need to check that the points of the triangles face the same direction. The easiest way is to lay out six triangle beads the same orientation, then pass the needle through the hole to the right of the bead each time **(fig. 10)**.

10 Stitch Row 5: Work the stitches over the tip beads of step 8, passing through the same hole of the triangle already used. The beads for this row are: 1xC (stalk) and 1xE (tip). Step up through the last stitch of the row **(fig. 11)**.

11 Spacer Row: For this row, pass through the second hole of the triangle beads and the tip beads of the last row **(fig. 12)**. Now you have reached the middle point of the section.

12 **Fig. 13–22** show the stitch rows and spacer rows to reverse the sequence. At the end of **fig. 22**, the spacer row is identical to the first base row in step 1.

13 Repeat the steps until the bracelet is the right length. The bracelets shown (p. 24) have six completed sections and measure 18cm (7 in.) without the clasp.
　　Attach the clasp as indicated on p. 19.

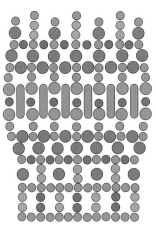

fig. 17

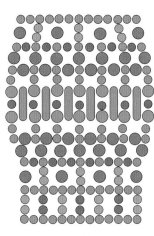

fig. 18

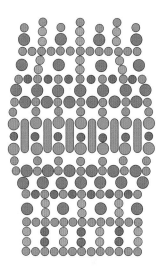

fig. 19

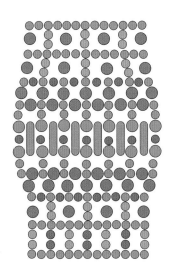

fig. 20

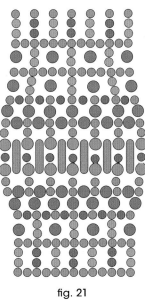

fig. 21

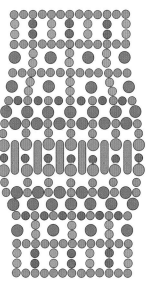

fig. 22

Slinky, elegant, and infinitely wearable, this design
showcases the adorable 2mm Czech pearl beads.
It shows how you can have different length stitches
within the same row to create a different kind of pattern.

Tea Dance

materials

11° seed beads

A 10g metallic dark bronze

B 10g opaque coral luster

C 10g opaque turquoise

D 10g matte dark blue

E 10g silver-lined teal

F 430 2mm Czech glass pearls, pea green

G 10 dagger beads, orange/lime mix

1 Secure a stop bead and pick up 9xA. Push the beads down to the stop bead **(fig. 1)**.

2 Basic Stitch Row: Pick up 1xB (stalk), 1xA (tip) **(fig. 2)**. At the end of the row, step up **(fig. 3)**.

3 Spacer Row: Place 1xA between each 1xA tip bead **(fig. 4)**.

4 Stitch Row 2: Each stitch has a different number of stalk beads; the number increases by one for each stitch.

  Stitch 1: 1xC (stalk); 1xA (tip)
  Stitch 2: 2xC (stalk); 1xA (tip)
  Stitch 3: 3xC (stalk); 1xA (tip)
  Stitch 4: 4xC (stalk); 1xA (tip)
  Stitch 5: 1xC, 1xB, 1xF, 1xB, 1xC (stalk); 1xA (tip)

  Step up through the beads of the fifth stitch to exit the tip bead **(fig. 5)**.

5 Spacer Row: 1xA between each 1xA tip bead. The long fifth stitch will curve slightly **(fig. 6 and 7)**.

6 Repeat steps 2 and 3, to add a basic stitch row and spacer row, but use 1xF stalk beads **(fig. 8 and 9)**.

note

2mm Czech pearls can be substituted with an alternative accent bead. 8° seed beads or 3mm crystals will also fit well within the stitches.

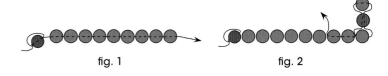

fig. 1   fig. 2

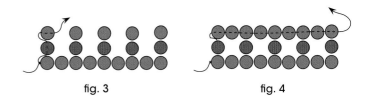

fig. 3   fig. 4

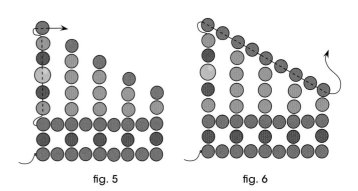

fig. 5   fig. 6

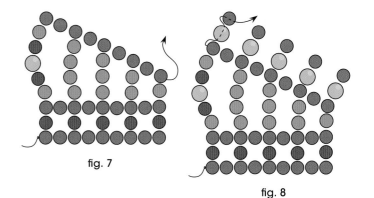

fig. 7   fig. 8

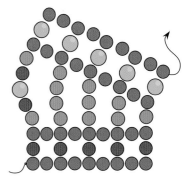

fig. 9

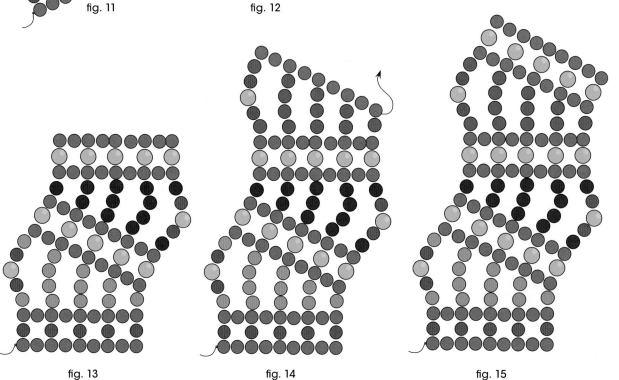

fig. 10

fig. 11

fig. 12

fig. 13

fig. 14

fig. 15

This lariat is a great project to experiment with colors. Add as many as you like. Try using beads of one color, but in different shades from dark to light. If you want to explore finishes, use one or two colors in matte, shiny opaque, transparent, and silver-lined.

7 Stitch Row 3: This is a mirror of Stitch Row 2, so it starts with the long stitch and decreases by one for each stitch. The bead color changes to the next color.

> Stitch 1: 1xE, 1xB, 1xF, 1xB, 1xE (stalk); 1xA (tip)
> Stitch 2: 4xE (stalk); 1xA (tip)
> Stitch 3: 3xE (stalk); 1xA (tip)
> Stitch 4: 2xE (stalk); 1xA (tip)
> Stitch 5: 1xE (stalk); 1xA (tip)

Step up through the beads to the fifth stitch to exit the tip bead **(fig. 10)**.

8 Repeat step 6 **(fig. 11** and **12)**.

9 Repeat step 3 **(fig. 13)**.

10 Repeat steps 4 and 5, but change the stalk bead color to F (the tips are always A). The long stitch keeps the sequence as before **(fig. 14)**.

Because the stitches change direction, you will create a length of beadwork that is relatively straight and the shaping will form a zigzag pattern of spacer rows.

To continue, keep the stitch pattern going: a basic row, a short to long row in the next color, and then a basic row followed by a long to short row in the next color **(fig. 15** and **16)**.

The lariat shown here measures 95cm (37.4 in.) without fringing.

Fig. 11–15 show the complete sequence using the four main colors. The sequence is then repeated until you have a length for a lariat, and ends with a basic row.

Fringe

The fringes are worked over alternate beads of the first and last row, and are basically a long stitch with a loop at the end instead of a tip bead.

Pick up 2xE, 2xF, 2xC, 1xB, 2xC, 2xF, 2xE, 2xA. Pick up this sequence one more time, and then again omitting the last 2xA.

Pick up 1xC 4xA, 1xG, 4xA. Pass back through the 1xC and all the remaining beads to get back to the base row. Pull the thread up gently **(fig. 17)**. Repeat to create four more fringes on this end.

Repeat on the other end of the lariat.

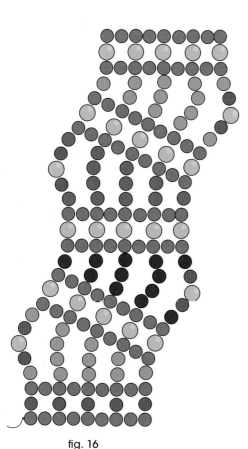

fig. 16

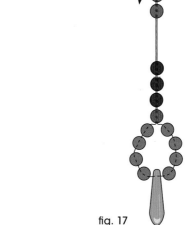

fig. 17

Not all rows need to be the same length—the Romantica cuff has mixed bead rows and introduces a simple surface embellishment to add a new texture. Stitches are placed over every third bead so there are two beads between each stitch and two beads for the spacer rows. The rows vary in length with a grid of three short rows separated with a row of much longer stitches

Romantica Cuff

materials

11º seed beads

A 8g matte frosted turquoise

B 8g coral pink Ceylon

C 8g dyed sea foam silver-lined alabaster

D 4g 15º seed beads, light gold metallic

E 80 3mm Czech pearls, light coral

F 40 3mm Czech fire-polished beads, crystal matte gold metallic

• 5-strand sliding clasp or similar, antique copper

note

The bracelets shown here have four short stitch sections, three row grid sections, and five long stitch sections, with a single short stitch section at each end. Without the clasp, they measure 19cm (7½ in.).

fig. 1

fig. 2

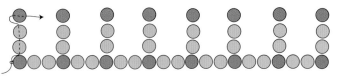

fig. 3

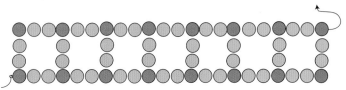

fig. 4

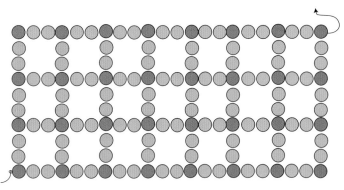

fig. 5

1 Secure a stop bead. Pick up 11º seed beads in this sequence: 1xB, 2xA until you have a total of 22 beads. End with 1xB. Push them down to the stop bead **(fig. 1)**.

2 Stitch 1: Pick up 2xA (stalk); 1xB (tip). Pass back through the 2xA, and pull up the thread. Step over the first B bead on the base row (the one the thread is coming from) and pass through the next three beads, (2xA, 1xB) of the base row. Pull up the thread. The first stitch should now sit at a right angle to the base row and over the end B bead **(fig. 2)**.

3 Stitches 2–8: Repeat step 2 to make a total of eight stitches (2xA/stalk, 1xB/tip) over the B beads of the base row. At the end of the row, remove the stop bead and secure the tail. Working the threads together, step up through the beads of the last stitch worked **(fig. 3)**.

4 Spacer Row: Pick up 2xA and pass through the next 1xB tip. Repeat to the end of the row. See how this gives a slightly different grid with almost square apertures **(fig. 4)**.

5 Repeat steps 2–4. You will have a three-row grid, ending with the spacer row of the third row of stitches **(fig. 5)**.

note

If you're not sure of the size, work a few sections: grid, long stitch. Switch back to the foundation row and work in the opposite direction (starting with a long stitch section). That way, you'll be able to see how many grid rows are needed to complete the ends of the bracelet. I beaded just one at each end.

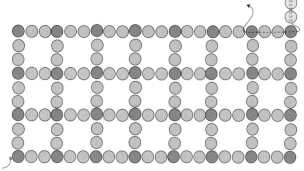

fig. 6

fig. 7

6 Row 5: These long stitches are worked in the same way, but have many more beads: 2xC, 1xB, 1xA, 1xD, 1xE, 1xD, 1xF, 1xD, 1xE, 1xD, 1xA, 1xB, 2xC (stalk); 1xB (tip). Make sure to pass back through all the stalk beads each time and come through 2xA, 1xB in the spacer row **(fig. 6)**.

Repeat to make a stitch above each B in the spacer row. At the end of the row, step up through the last stitch.

7 Spacer Row: Pick up 2xA spacer beads between each 1xB tip bead **(fig. 7)**.

Now you are in place to add three more rows of stitches as before with 2xA stalks and 1xB tips, and spacer rows of 2xA between each tip bead.

Embellishing the Grid

I use this cute embellishment often in my Albion stitch projects. There are several variations, of which this is the easiest. Use it to embellish across the central row of each three-row grid section and the end rows. Look at the grid. There are square apertures, each with four 2xB sides and four 1xA corners. The embellishment lies over the aperture.

1 Exit a top 1xB in the right corner of the end aperture of the center row of a grid section.

Pick up 1xD, 1xC, 1xD. Pass through the 2xA spacer beads at the bottom of the same aperture **(fig. 8)**.

2 Pick up 1xD, pass through the 1xC of step one, pick up 1xD, pass through the 1xB top left corner bead of the aperture **(fig. 9)**. You are now in place to repeat the steps for the next aperture.

3 Complete the row of embellishment **(fig. 10)**. Then, either finish off the thread, or weave through the rows to embellish the next grid section.

Stitch a clasp to the end rows to complete the bracelet.

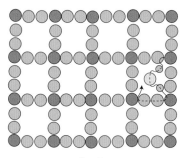

fig. 8

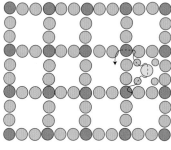

fig. 9

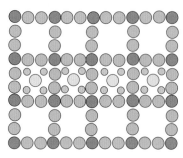

fig. 10

Tubular Albion Stitch

Now we take a look at tubular Albion stitch. Instead of a row of beads, the base row is a ring of beads. Increasing and shaping can be added in the same was as they can be for the flat form of the stitch. Tubular Albion stitch can be used to make pretty beaded beads and is the starting point for working three-dimensional designs.

COLOR INSPIRATION

Market garden is the inspiration for this color mix. It starts with fresh ginger and leafy greens. You can add any powdered spice colors, like cinnamon and mustard, or the paler colors of sliced celery and lemons. The perfect companion to these colors is a cool lavender or violet. If you are yearning for a bit more richness in this delicate mix, look for the darker tones of ripe plum, grape, or beetroot.

The Magic Lantern beads explore how to make gentle increases and use a mix of bead sizes and shapes. The beads are hollow, and will get you used to a firmer thread tension. If you know that your thread tension is on the soft side, pass right round each spacer row a second time to tighten things up as you go.

Magic Lanterns

materials

- **A** 5g 15º seed beads, violet silver-lined

11º seed beads
- **B** 6g color-lined purple
- **C** 6g color-lined pale yellow
- **D** 6g ginger brown silky silver-lined

- **E** 5g 8º seed beads, ginger brown silky silver-lined

- **F** 76 two-hole SuperDuo beads

- 2 1-meter lengths of rolled silk ribbon or similar

fig. 1

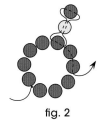
fig. 2

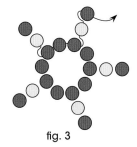
fig. 3

Make a Lantern

1 Pick up 10xB and secure them in a ring. Exit a bead **(fig. 1)**.

2 Stitches 1–5: Place a stitch, 1xC (stalk) and 1xB (tip), over alternate beads on the ring. Step up through the first stitch worked **(fig. 2** and **3)**.

3 Spacer Round: Pick up 1xB between each 1xB tip bead from step 2 **(fig. 4)**. Viewed from above, this now forms a new base ring for the next round of stitches **(fig. 5** shows top and side views).

4 Stitch Round: Place a stitch over each bead in the new base ring: 1xB, 1xE (stalk); 1xF (tip). Use just one hole of the two-hole F bead **(fig. 6** and **7)**. At the end of the round, step up to exit the tip bead of the first stitch worked in this round. This is an increase round so you should have 10 stitches **(fig. 8)**.

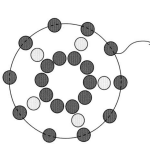
fig. 4

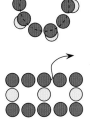

fig. 5

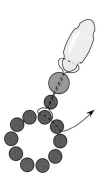
fig. 6

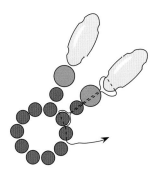
fig. 7

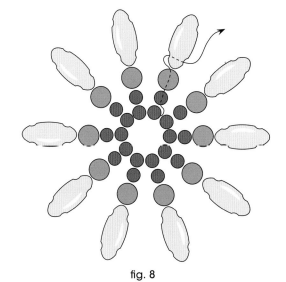
fig. 8

note

I used hand-dyed rolled silk ribbon from an Etsy artisan. An alternative is rattail cord, which comes in a great selection of colors.

5 Spacer Round: Pick up 1xB between each 1xF tip bead, passing through the same hole of the two-hole F already in use **(fig. 9)**.

6 Stitch Round: Place a stitch over each spacer bead from step 5: 1xA, 1xD, 1xA (stalk); 1xB (tip) **(fig. 10)**. At the end of the round, step up through the first stitch worked in this round **(fig. 11)**.

    These stitches are longer than the F beads. As you work the next round, allow them to bend in the middle. As the round is pulled up, allow the F beads to move inwards, and the bent stitches to move outwards. Once the round is secure, they will stay in this formation.

7 Instead of adding a spacer round, pass through the second hole of the F bead and the tip beads of the stitches alternately. Pull the thread firmly, and pass through the beads a second time to tighten this round. Bring the needle out of a B bead **(fig. 12** and **13)**.

    Now you are past the widest part of the beaded bead and in place to start the decrease to mirror the first two rounds.

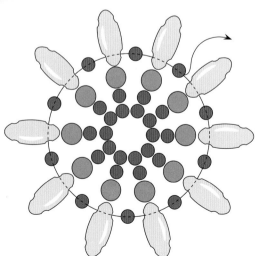

fig. 9

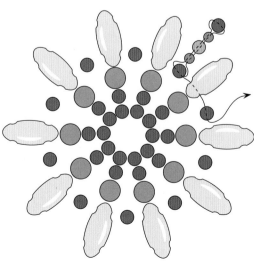

fig. 10

8 Stitch Round: The 10 stitches for this round sit over the ends of the F beads; the needle will pass through only the B beads as you complete each stitch: 1xE (stalk); 1xB (tip) **(fig. 14)**. At the end of the round, step up to exit the first stitch tip bead **(fig. 15)**.

9 Instead of adding a spacer round, pass the needle through each tip bead. Pull the thread firmly. This now forms a new base ring of 10xB. Bring the needle out of a tip bead **(fig. 16)**.

10 Stitch Round: Place a stitch over each tip bead in the base ring: Pick up 1xC (stalk); 1xA (tip).

11 Spacer Round: Pick up 1xB between each A tip bead **(fig. 17)**. Now the beaded bead is complete. Finish off any thread tails.

Make three more beaded beads. Make a larger center bead by following the same steps, but starting with a base ring of 32xB.

To make two end caps for the ribbon, follow steps 1–7, then finish off the thread tails.

Put it Together

String four beaded beads over two strands of silk ribbon.

Pass one set of ribbon ends through the big bead from left to right, and pass the other set of ribbon ends from right to left.

Straighten the ribbons so the ends match up. Thread an end cap (half bead) on to one set of ribbon ends. Knot the ribbon ends and pull the end cap over the knot to hide it. Repeat at the other end of the ribbons.

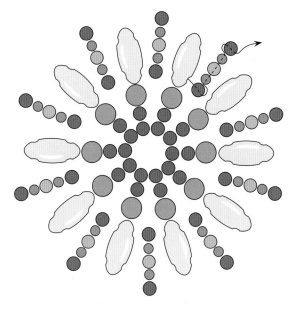

fig. 11

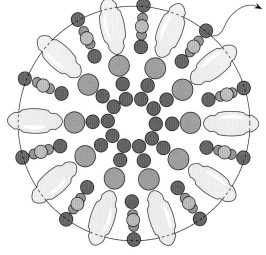

fig. 12

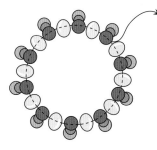

fig. 13

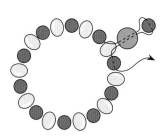

fig. 14

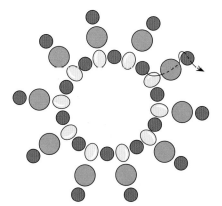

fig. 15

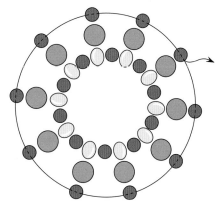

fig. 16

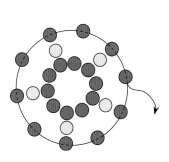

fig. 17

The Tapestry Tails lariat is a design that can be infinitely adapted. The pattern given here is a basic recipe. Like all great cooks, feel free to add your own ingredients and variations on the stitch sequence. Each stitch is worked in a sequence to create a repeating pattern of stitches, beads, and colors. It's a great way to bring lots of different beads and colors together.

Tapestry Tails

materials

11º seed beads

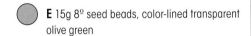
A 15g ginger brown silky silver-lined

B 15g color-lined purple

C 15g violet silver silky-lined

D 15g silver-lined transparent olive green

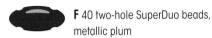
E 15g 8º seed beads, color-lined transparent olive green

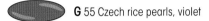
F 40 two-hole SuperDuo beads, metallic plum

G 55 Czech rice pearls, violet

H 150 3mm Czech crystals, matte metallic copper

- 10 accent beads for fringe tip (the design shown uses Czech glass square beads)

This will make a lariat 100cm (39 in.) long (including fringe). For a longer lariat, increase accent bead quantities in multiples of five.

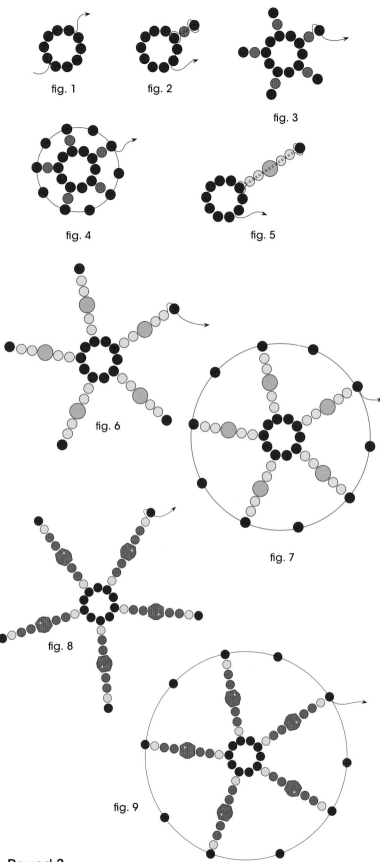

fig. 1

fig. 2

fig. 3

fig. 4

fig. 5

fig. 6

fig. 7

fig. 8

fig. 9

Round Sequence

Work Rounds 1, 2, 3, 4, 3, 2, 5, and 2. Repeat the sequence seven more times. Then work Rounds 3, 4, 3, 2, and 1.

Base Round

Pick up 10xB and secure them in a ring. Exit a bead on the ring **(fig. 1)**.

Round 1

1 Stitch Round: Stitch over alternate beads on the ring: 1xC (stalk); 1xB (tip) **(fig 2)**. Step up to exit the tip bead of the first stitch **(fig. 3)**.

2 Spacer Round: Pick up 1xB between each tip bead. Complete the round and exit a tip bead **(fig. 4)**.

Round 2

1 Stitch Round: Place a stitch over the tip beads of the base round: 2xD, 1xE, 2xD (stalk); 1xB (tip) **(fig. 5)**. Step up to exit the tip bead of the first stitch **(fig. 6)**.

2 Spacer Round: Pick up 1xB between each tip bead. Complete the round and exit a tip bead **(fig. 7)**.

Round 3

1 Stitch Round: Place a stitch over the tip beads of the base round: 1xD, 2xA, 1xH, 2xA, 1xD (stalk); 1xB (tip). Step up to exit the tip bead of the first stitch **(fig. 8)**.

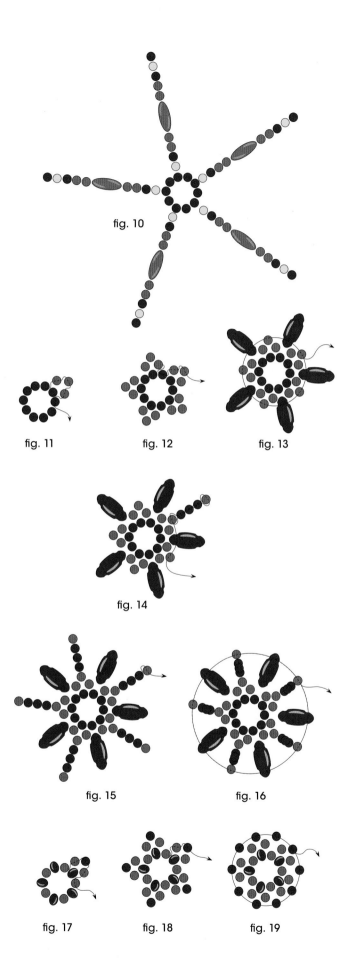

fig. 10

fig. 11

fig. 12

fig. 13

fig. 14

fig. 15

fig. 16

fig. 17

fig. 18

fig. 19

2 Spacer Round: Pick up 1xB between each tip bead. Complete the round and exit a tip bead **(fig. 9)**.

Round Four

1 Stitch Round: Place a stitch over tip beads of the base round: 1xD, 1xB, 2xC, 1xG, 2xC, 1xB, 1xD (stalk); 1xB (tip). Step up to exit the tip bead of the first stitch **(fig. 10)**.

2 Spacer Round: Pick up 1xB between each tip bead. Complete the round and exit a tip bead.

Round Five

1 This round is a little different. Pick up 3xA. Pass through the next tip bead on the base round **(fig. 11)**. Repeat all the way around (five sets of 3xA). At the end of the round, step up through the first two beads of the first 3xA added **(fig. 12)**.

2 Spacer Round: Pick up 1xF between each center bead of the 3xA sets, using just one hole of the F bead. At the end of the round, exit a center A bead **(fig. 13)**.

3 Stitch Round: Place a stitch over each center A of the previous round: 3xB (stalk); 1xA (tip) **(fig. 14)**. At the end of the round, step up to exit the tip bead of the first stitch worked in this round **(fig. 15)**.

4 Spacer Round: Pass through the second hole of the F bead and the 1xA tip beads alternately. The stitches need to gently fold outwards and the F beads slide inwards. Pass through the beads a second time to secure this round firmly. Exit a tip bead **(fig. 16)**.

5 Stitch Round: Pick up 1xA, 1xB, 1xA, and pass through the next tip bead of the previous round **(fig. 17)**. Repeat all the way around. At the end of the round, step up through the first 1xA and 1xB added in this round **(fig. 18)**.

6 Spacer Round: Pick up 1xB between each center B bead of the sets. At the end of the round, exit a center B bead **(fig. 19)**.

Repeat the sequence of rounds seven more times. Complete the lariat with: Rounds 3, 4, 3, 2, and 1.

Fringe

Work fringes from alternate beads of the end rows. For an accent bead at the end, use daggers, droplets, or any shaped bead with a hole at one end.

Each fringe is: 3xA, 2xD, 1xB, 1xE, 1xB, 2xD, 2xA, 1xH, 2xA, 2xD, 1xB, 1xG, 1xB, 2xD, 2xA, 2xB, 2xD, 1xB, 1xH, 1xB, 3xB, accent bead, 3xB. Skip the 3xB, accent bead, and 3xB and pass back through all of the remaining beads.

Add five fringes to each end of the lariat.

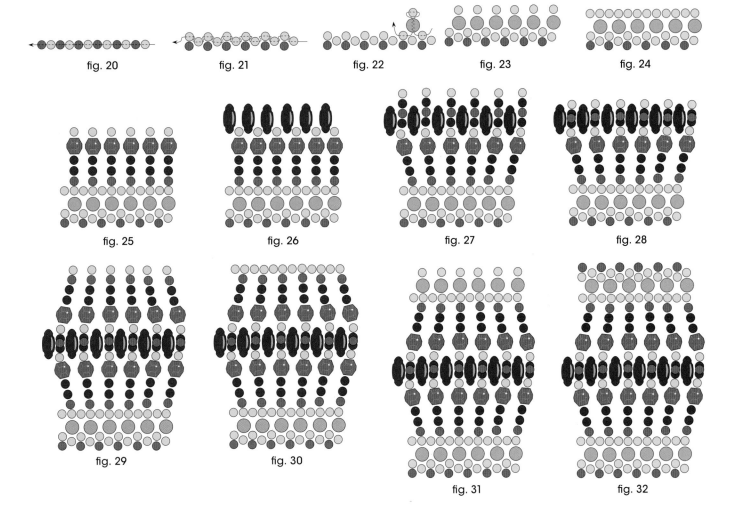

fig. 20   fig. 21   fig. 22   fig. 23   fig. 24

fig. 25   fig. 26   fig. 27   fig. 28

fig. 29   fig. 30   fig. 31   fig. 32

The Slider Bead

This tube pattern is shown as a flat diagram. The diagrams show just one section of the entire round.

1 Pick up 30 11º seed beads, alternating A and D **(fig. 20)**. Secure the beads in a ring and exit a D.

2 Peyote stitch one round using D beads. The Ds will sit over the As **(fig. 21)**.

3 Stitch Round: Between the D beads of the previous round, place: 1xE (stalk); 1xD (tip) **(fig. 22** and **23)**.

4 Spacer Round: Place 1xD between each 1xD tip bead **(fig. 24)**.

5 Stitch Round: Place a stitch over each tip bead of the previous round: 1xA, 2xB, 1xH (stalk); 1xD (tip) **(fig. 25)**.

6 Spacer Round: Place 1xF between each 1xD tip bead, using one hole of the F bead **(fig. 26)**.

7 Stitch Round: Place a stitch over each tip bead: 1xA, 1xB, 1xA (stalk); 1xD (tip) **(fig. 27)**.

8 Spacer Round: Pass through alternate tip beads and the second holes of F beads. Allow the stitches to fold outwards and the F beads to slide inwards. Secure the round **(fig. 28)**.

9 Stitch Round: Place a stitch over the tip beads of the previous round: 1xH, 2xB, 1xA (stalk); 1xD (tip) **(fig. 29)**.

10 Spacer Round: Pick up 1xD between each 1xD tip bead **(fig. 30)**.

11 Stitch Round: Place a stitch over each tip bead of the previous round: 1xE, (stalk); 1xD (tip) **(fig. 31)**.

12 Spacer Round: Pick up 1xD between each 1xD tip bead **(fig. 32)**.

13 Peyote stitch one round using A beads, passing through the tip beads so the A beads sit over the spacer beads of the previous round **(fig. 33)**. Finish off the thread tails.

Slide the bead on to the lariat by threading one end of the lariat through at a time.

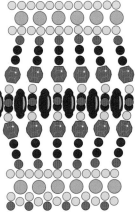

fig. 33

Short sections of tubular Albion stitch can be used to make cute tassels and necklace sides. This design uses a repeating motif and introduces the technique for building from a spacer row to create simple loops.

Textured Tassel

materials

11º seed beads

A 10g silver-lined transparent purple

B 10g color-lined purple

C 10g violet silky silver-lined

D 10g color-lined transparent olive green

E 10g silver-lined transparent lime

F 6g 8º seed beads, lime silky silver-lined

G 72 Magatamas, transparent violet AB

- 25mm Polaris acrylic ring, lime green
- 2 5mm jump rings
- small lobster clasp

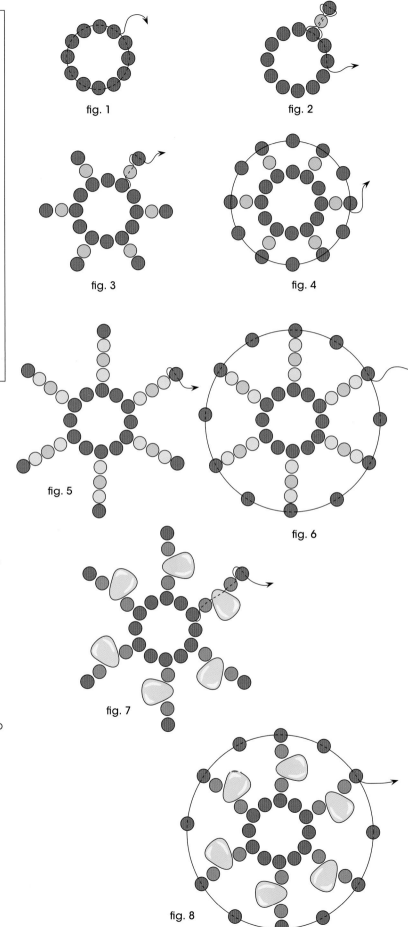

fig. 1

fig. 2

fig. 3

fig. 4

fig. 5

fig. 6

fig. 7

fig. 8

This design is worked as a series of repeating rounds.

Round 1

1 Pick up 12xC and secure in a ring. Exit through a bead on the ring **(fig. 1)**.

2 Place a stitch over alternate beads on the ring: 1xE (stalk); 1xC (tip) **(fig. 2)**. Step up to exit the tip bead of the first stitch **(fig. 3)**.

3 Spacer Round: Pick up 1xC between each 1xC tip bead **(fig. 4)**.

Round 2

1 Place a stitch over each tip bead of the previous round: 1xD, 1xE, 1xD (stalk); 1xC (tip) **(fig. 5)**.

2 Spacer Round: Pick up 1xC between each tip bead. Exit the tip bead of the first stitch **(fig. 6)**.

Round 3

1 Place a stitch over the tip beads of the previous round: 1xB, 1xG, 1xB (stalk); 1xC (tip). Step up to exit the tip bead of the first stitch **(fig. 7)**.

2 Spacer Round: Pick up 1xC between each 1xC tip bead. Exit the tip bead of the first stitch **(fig. 8)**. Nudge the magatama beads so they point outwards. Once the round is secure they will stay in place.

fig. 9

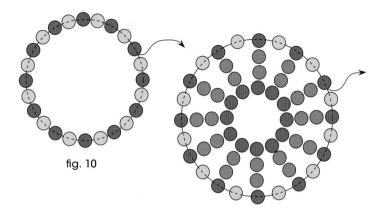

fig. 10

fig. 11

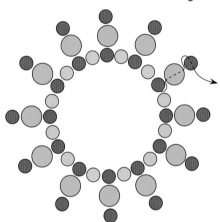

fig. 12

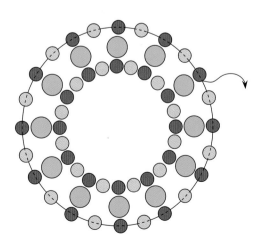

fig. 13

Round 4

1 Place a stitch over a spacer bead: 2xB (stalk); 1xC (tip) **(fig. 9)**. Repeat over every bead of the spacer round (12 stitches).

2 Spacer Round: Pick up 1xA between each 1xC tip bead **(fig. 10** and **11)**.

Round 5

1 Place a stitch over each tip bead of the previous round: 1xF (stalk); 1xC (tip) **(fig. 12)**.

2 Spacer Round: 1xA between each 1xC tip bead **(fig. 13)**.

Round 6

1 Place a stitch over each tip bead of the previous round: 2xB (stalk); 1xC (tip) **(fig. 14)**.

2 Instead of a spacer round, just pass through all the tip beads and secure the ring **(fig. 15)**.

Round Sequences

To make the necklace sides, work the rounds in this sequence:
Rounds 1, 2; 1, 3–6, 3, 1, 2, 2 (changing 1xD, 1xE, 1xD, to 1xB, 1xC, 1xB), 2, 1, 3–6, 3, and 1.
Make two.

Tassel (Make One)

Work the rounds in this sequence:
Rounds 1, 3–6, 3, 4, and 5.
Add a fringe to each bead of the Round 6 spacer round, giving 12 fringes.
Each fringe is: 2xD, 1xB, 1xC, 1xA, 1xC, 1xB, 2xD, 1xE, 1xF, 1xE. Repeat, and then pick up 2xD, 1xB, 1xC, 1xA, 1xC, 1xB, 1xF, 3xC, Magatama, 3xC. Pass back through all the beads except 3xC, Magatama, 3xC.

End loops

Each necklace section has two end loops. One end is used to support a stand of seed beads, the other is worked around an acrylic ring. The tassel has one loop worked around the ring.
Start with the necklace ends, which are simpler. Then, the loops that are stitched with the ring in place will be a breeze. On one end of each necklace section:

1 Bring the needle out of a bead on the end spacer round. Pick up 15xC, pass the needle through the fourth bead around from the start point on the base round **(fig. 16)**.

2 Pass back through the 15xC, the base round bead started from, and 2xC of the 15xC. You are now in place to put a stitch over this and alternate beads of the 15xC **(fig. 17)**.

3 Place a stitch over alternate beads of the loop of 15xC: 1xE (stalk); 1xC (tip). At the end of the round, pass through the last bead of the 15xA and three beads on the base round **(fig. 18)**.

4 Pick up 1xC, pass through the nearest 1xC tip bead. Place 1xC between each tip bead. At the end of the round, pick up 1xC and pass through the bead marked with a black dot **(fig. 19)**. Pass back through all the beads of the spacer row again, then finish off the thread.

On the other end of each necklace section, and the top of the tassel section:

5 Follow the loop steps 1–4, but at step 1, make sure the 15xC is strung through the Polaris ring **(fig. 20)**. Work with the ring in place for each of these connecting loops.

I've used a simple strand of seed beads, repeating the pattern in the fringing. It is long enough to thread through the end loops of the necklace sides. Behind the neck, I added a lobster clasp and jump rings. Start the strand with a loop of beads through a jump ring thread on the beads, and end with a loop through a second jump ring. I used a second strand of thread to repeat the thread path and to make the strand of beads nice and strong.

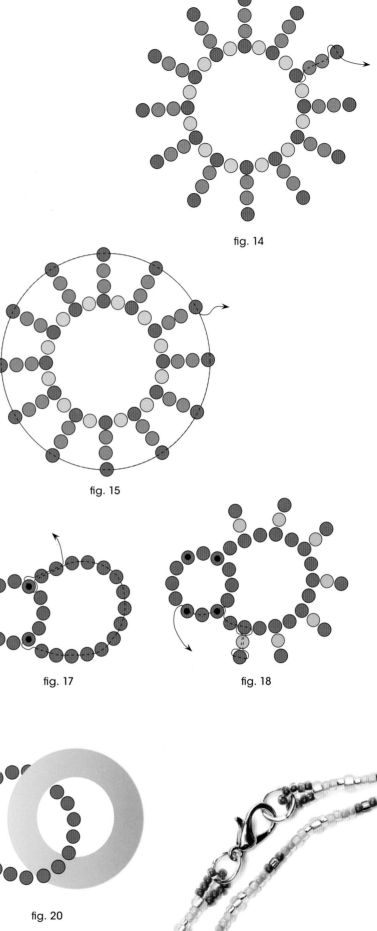

fig. 14

fig. 15

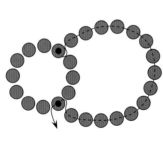

fig. 16

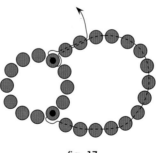

fig. 17

fig. 18

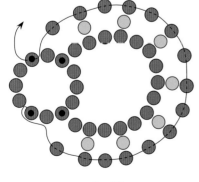

fig. 19

fig. 20

A bangle is a really big, but very short, tube. Jangle bangles expand on the idea of building from a row to build a box section tube. It is firm, but flexible enough to slide over the hand.

Jangle Bangle

materials

 A 4g 15º seed beads, color-lined transparent olive green

 11º seed beads
B 15g color-lined transparent purple
C 5g silver-lined transparent purple

D 4g 8º seed beads, color-lined transparent olive green

E 23 6mm two-hole pyramid beads

note

The illustrations show a tiny ring in comparison to actual size, just so that the diagrams will fit on the pages. Once the base is done, the diagrams show just a section of the whole.

1 To make the base ring, pick up B beads in multiples of three until you have enough beads to form a ring which will slide over the widest part of your hand. Secure the beads into a ring and exit a bead **(fig. 1)**.

2 Place a stitch over every third bead on the ring: 2xB (stalk); 1xB (tip). Step up to exit the tip bead of the first stitch **(fig. 2)**.

3 Spacer Round: Pick up 2xB between each 1xA tip bead. Exit a tip bead once the round is secure **(fig. 3)**.

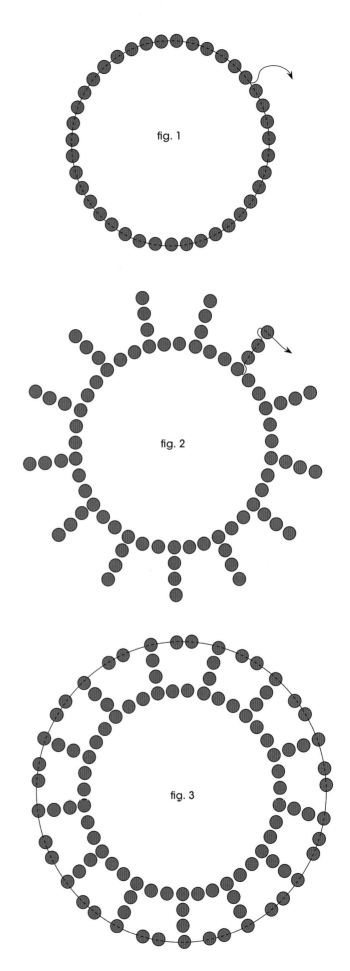

fig. 1

fig. 2

fig. 3

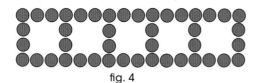

fig. 4

Viewed from the side, you now have a band of beadwork with a base round at each side and stalk beads across the center **(fig. 4)**.

4 Place a stitch over each tip bead of the base round: 2xB (stalk); 1xB (tip) **(fig. 5)**.

At the end of the round, instead of stepping up through the last stitch, weave through the beadwork to the other side of the base and exit a tip bead.

5 Place a stitch over each tip bead of the base round: 2xB (stalk); 1xB (tip) **(fig. 6)**.

At the end of the round, step up to exit the tip bead of the first stitch worked in this round.

6 Spacer Round: Pick up 1xC and 1xE alternately between the tip beads. Note: the stitches will distort slightly to accommodate the E beads. Weave through this round a second time to secure it **(fig. 7)**.

7 Weave through the beads to exit a tip bead of the row of beads worked in step 4. Repeat step 6, making sure the stitches line up and are passing through the second hole of the E beads **(fig. 8** and **9)**.

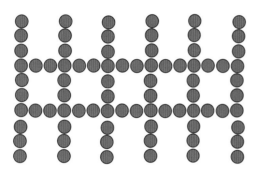

fig. 5

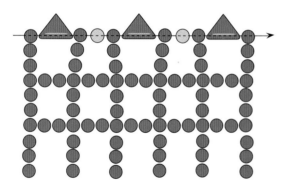

fig. 6

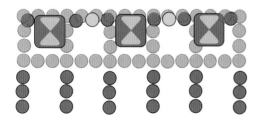

fig. 7

note

Make sure to pick up the E beads so they will sit face-up across the bangle when the second spacer row is added (through the second hole of the E beads).

fig. 8

fig. 9

Embellishing the Bangle

Both the sides and the top between the E beads have embellishment details. These give the bangle more body and more strength.

For the top embellishment, the thread passes through the E beads:

1 Exit an E bead, pick up 1xA, 1xD, 1xA, and pass through the next E bead. Repeat all the way around, then step up by passing through 1xA, 1xD of the first set of beads added **(fig. 10)**.

fig. 10

2 Pick up 1xA and pass through the second hole of the E bead. Pick up 1xA and pass through the next 1xD. Repeat all the way around the bangle. At the end of the round, bring the needle through to exit an E bead and then pass through the 1xB after the E bead on the bangle edge **(fig. 11)**.

fig. 11

Side Embellishment

(Repeat on both sides.) This embellishment is slightly three dimensional so the bangle is wider at the top edge.

1 Exit a tip bead before an end bead, and pick up 1xB, 2xA, 1xC, 1xB. Pass through the 2xB spacer beads of the bottom edge **(fig. 12)**.

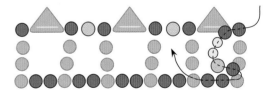

fig. 12

2 Pick up 1xA, and pass through the 1xC and 1xA of step 1. Pick up 1xA and pass through the A bead after the E bead on the top edge. You are now in place to repeat the embellishment over the next aperture **(fig. 13)**.

Repeat all the way around the bangle **(fig. 14)**, then weave to the other side to add the same embellishment.

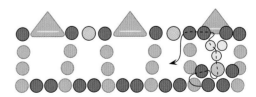

fig. 13

note

I've used a simple color selection, but feel free to add in more colors. If you don't like the spikiness of pyramid beads and would prefer a softer design, substitute CzechMate two-hole Tile beads.

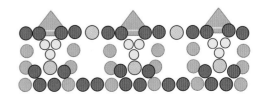

fig. 14

Of all the ways to use Albion stitch, making bezels is one of my favorites. Boiled Candy is a fun way to create double-sided bezel cabochons, all strung together on an Albion stitch ribbon. I've used these to make all sorts of different necklace shapes, but I return to the elegance of a lariat for this example.

Boiled Candy

materials

15º seed beads

- **A** 6g dyed pumpkin
- **B** 6g color-lined transparent olive green

11º seed beads

- **C** 15g silver-lined pale celery
- **D** 15g ginger brown silky silver-lined
- **E** 15g color-lined transparent dark olive

- **F** 68 4mm Swarovski bicone crystals, lime
- **6** 18mm Soft Touch cabochons, olive and ginger

Miyuki seed beads are best for this design.

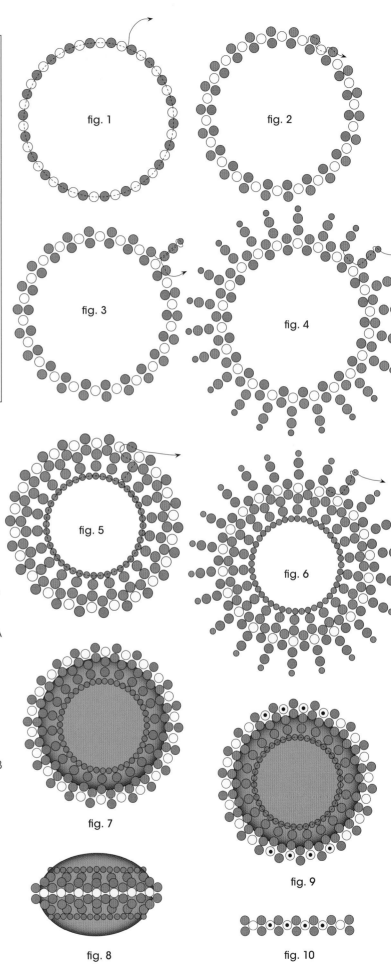

fig. 1

fig. 2

fig. 3

fig. 4

fig. 5

fig. 6

fig. 7

fig. 8

fig. 9

fig. 10

1 Pick up 44 11º seed beads, alternating C and D. Secure the beads in a ring and bring the needle out of a C bead **(fig. 1)**.

2 Peyote stitch one round using E beads, which will sit over the D beads. At the end of the round, step up to exit the first E bead added **(fig. 2)**.

3 Place a stitch between the E beads: 2xE (stalk); 1xA (tip) **(fig. 3)**. At the end of the round, step up to exit an A tip bead **(fig. 4)**.

4 Spacer Round: Pick up 1xB between each 1xA tip bead. Pull the thread up and the stitches will fold over to form the first half of the bezel. Weave through the beads to exit a D on the base round **(fig. 5)**.

5 Place a stitch between each 1xD: 2xD (stalk); 1xB (tip) **(fig. 5)**.

6 Spacer Round: Pick up 1xA between each 1xB tip bead. Before pulling the round tight, place two cabochons (back to back) into the bezel. Pull the round tight and weave through the beads of the round a second time to secure it **(fig. 7**, top, **fig. 8**, side).
    Repeat to make a total of six pieces.

The Ribbon Sequence

The bezels are linked through the center (C bead) row of peyote stitch. Each ribbon section has three stitches, so use four C beads on the bezel. The beads are marked with a black dot in **fig. 10 (fig. 9** and **10)**.

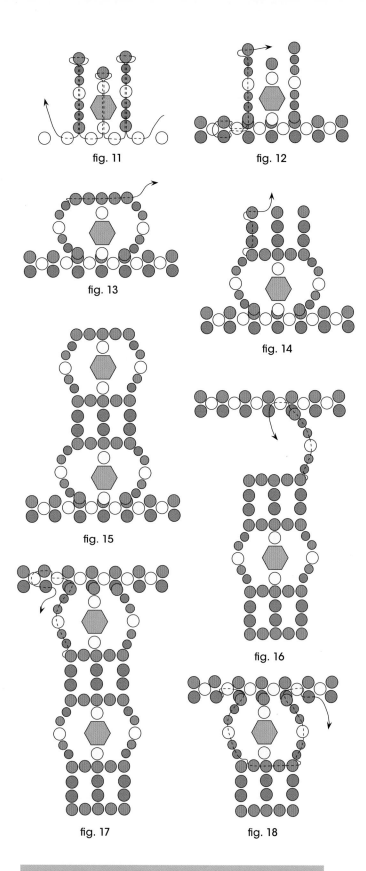

fig. 11

fig. 12

fig. 13

fig. 14

fig. 15

fig. 16

fig. 17

fig. 18

1 Exit a C bead on a bezel, and pick up: 1xE, 1xA, 1xB, 1xC, 1xB, 1xA (stalk); 1xE (tip). Pass back through the stalk beads and through the next C bead on the bezel.

Pick up: 1xC, 1xF, 1xC (stalk); 1xE (tip). Pass back through the stalk and the next 1xC.

Pick up: 1xE, 1xA, 1xB, 1xC, 1xB, 1xA (stalk); 1xE (tip). Pass back through the stalk beads and through the next C bead on the bezel **(fig. 11)**.

2 To turn through the beadwork, pass through 1xD of the peyote row, then turn and pass through 1xE and the 1xC started from. Now you are in place to step up through the last stitch worked and exit the tip bead **(fig. 12)**.

3 Spacer Row: Pick up 1xE between each 1xE tip bead **(fig. 13)**. The two outside stitches will curve slightly to line up with the shorter center stitch.

4 Place a stitch over each tip bead of the spacer row: 2xD (stalk); 1xE (tip) **(fig. 14)**.

5 Spacer Row: Pick up 1xE between each 1xE tip bead **(fig. 15)**.

Repeat the stitches so you have three crystal rows and three 2xD rows.

6 Join the ribbon to the next bezel: Pick up 1xA, 1xB, 1xC, 1xB, 1xA (stalk); 1xE (tip). Pass through the stalk and 1xC on the next bezel edge **(fig. 16)**. Pick up 1xE, 1xC, 1xF, 1xC (stalk). Pass back through the stalk beads and the beads of the spacer row to exit the end bead. Pick up 1xA, 1xB, 1xC, 1xB, 1xA (stalk); 1xE (tip). Pass back through the stalk and 1xC on the bezel. Turn through the beads of the bezel as before **(fig. 17)**.

7 Follow the thread path back through the beads to secure the stitches in the opposite direction. Weave through the beads of the bezel edge to the opposite side to start the next section of ribbon **(fig. 18)**.

Join a bezel, then repeat the short ribbon sequence to join the final two bezels.

When three bezels are joined, continue the ribbon until you have worked 51 crystal rows separated with 2xD bead rows, ending with a 2xD bead row.

note

The lemon and violet version has been put together with lemon showing on one side and violet on the other, giving you two variations in one lariat.

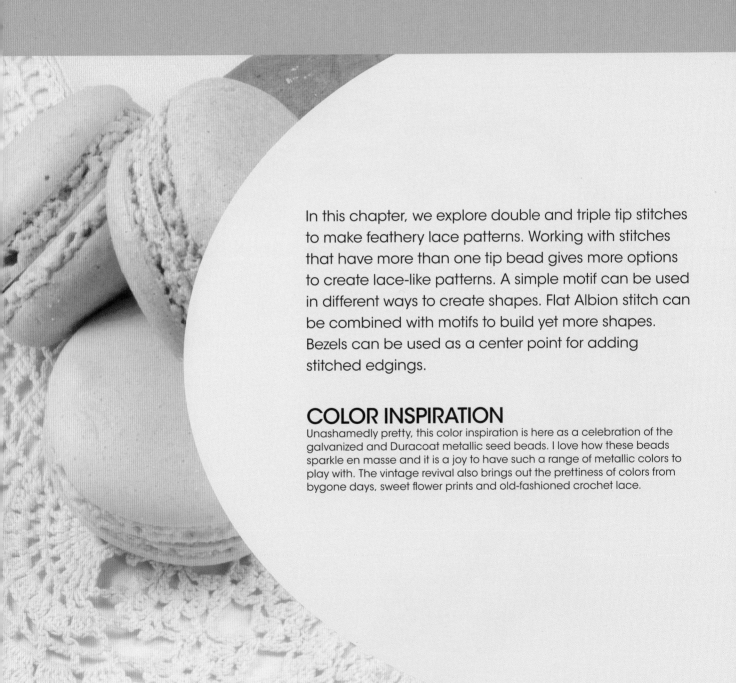

Ribbons and Lace

In this chapter, we explore double and triple tip stitches to make feathery lace patterns. Working with stitches that have more than one tip bead gives more options to create lace-like patterns. A simple motif can be used in different ways to create shapes. Flat Albion stitch can be combined with motifs to build yet more shapes. Bezels can be used as a center point for adding stitched edgings.

COLOR INSPIRATION

Unashamedly pretty, this color inspiration is here as a celebration of the galvanized and Duracoat metallic seed beads. I love how these beads sparkle en masse and it is a joy to have such a range of metallic colors to play with. The vintage revival also brings out the prettiness of colors from bygone days, sweet flower prints and old-fashioned crochet lace.

When I first developed this technique, I was very excited to be able to work long lengths of interlinked motifs without having to make lots of little pieces. Play around with this design as it will easily adapt to include all sorts of accent beads. It is ideal for long lariats, but also lies nicely as shorter strands.

Cloister Ribbon

materials

11º seed beads

A 10g Duracoat teal

B 10g matte frosted turquoise

C 5g 1.8mm Miyuki cube beads, color-lined turquoise

D 10g 8º seed beads, galvanized matte light green

E 68 3mm Czech fire-polished opaque turquoise AB

F 20 CzechMate two-hole lentils, opaque pale green AB

- 2 6mm jump rings
- lobster claw clasp

Each motif uses 4xE and 4xD; each link section uses 1xF and 2xD.

Motif

1 Pick up 8xA and secure in a ring. Exit through a bead **(fig. 1)**.

2 Place a stitch over the bead the thread exits: 1xE, 1xB (stalk); 3xA (tip). Pass through two beads of the base ring **(fig. 2)**.

3 Repeat step 2 **(fig. 3 and 4)** until you have four stitches sitting over alternate beads of the base ring. Step up to exit the third tip bead of the first stitch worked in step 2 **(fig. 5)**.

4 Pick up 2xB, 1xA, 1xD. Pass through the bead on the base ring between the first and second stitch. Then, pass back through the 1xD **(fig. 6)**.

5 Pick up 1xA, 2xB, and pass through the center and third tip bead of the next stitch **(fig. 7)**.

6 Repeat steps 4 and 5 **(fig. 8)** until you get back to the beginning. Exit the center tip bead of the first stitch **(fig. 9)**. This completes the first motif.

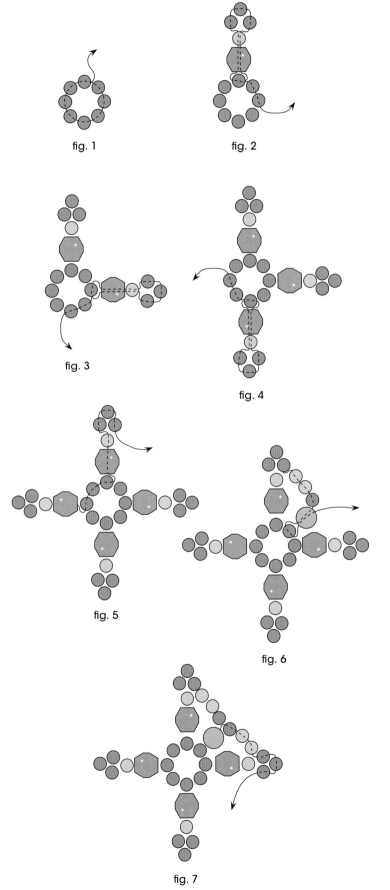

fig. 1

fig. 2

fig. 3

fig. 4

fig. 5

fig. 6

fig. 7

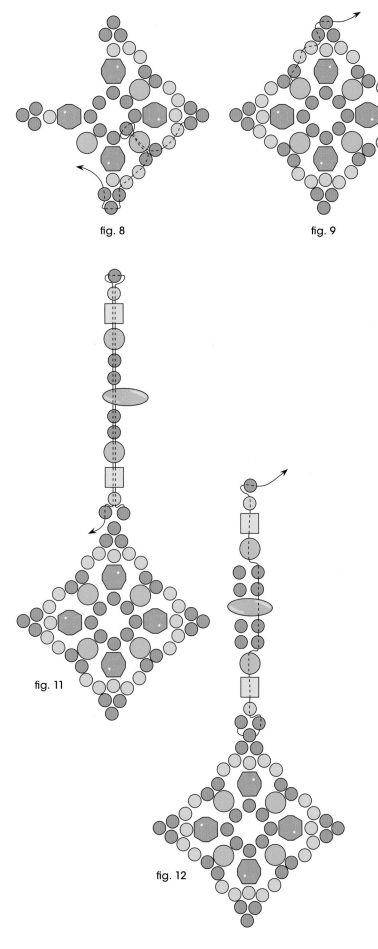

fig. 8

fig. 9

fig. 10

fig. 11

fig. 12

Link

7 Pick up 2xA and pass back through the 1xA center tip bead of the first stitch and the first of the 2xA just added **(fig. 10)**.

8 Pick up 1xB, 1xC, 1xD, 2xA, 1xF, 2xA, 1xD, 1xC, 1xB (stalk); 1xA (tip). Pass back through all the stalk beads and the second A bead of the 2xA added in step 7. Pull the thread to make sure the beads are secure **(fig. 11)**.

9 Pass through the center tip bead and the first A bead of the 2xA added in step 7. Pass back up through 1xB, 1xC, 1xD. Pick up 2xA, pass through the second hole of the F bead, and pick up 2xA. Then, pass through the remaining 1xD, 1xC, 1xB and the 1xA tip bead. Pull the thread again to settle the beads so the stitch is secure **(fig. 12)**. This completes the first link section.

Motif

Begin a new motif. The placement of the stitches is in a specific order so that you will be in place to make the next link section once this new motif is completed.

10 Pick up 2xA and pass back through the tip bead and 1xA of the 2xA just added **(fig. 13)**.

11 Make a stitch: 1xB, 1xE (stalk), 1xA (tip). Pass back through the stalk beads and the second A of the 2xA added in step 10 **(fig. 14)**. Pass through the tip bead and the first bead of the 2xA. Pass back up through the stalk beads and exit the 1xA tip bead **(fig. 15)**.

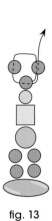

fig. 13

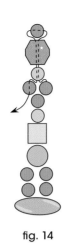

fig. 14

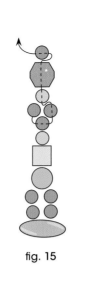

fig. 15

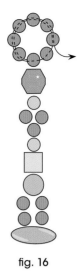

fig. 16

12 Pick up 7xA and pass back through the 1xA tip bead. Pass through 6xA of the 7xA **(fig. 16)**.

13 Place a stitch over the sixth bead: 1xE, 1xB (stalk); 3xA (tip). Pass back through the sixth bead of the base ring. Pass through the seventh bead, the tip bead started from in step 11, then on through two more beads of the base ring **(fig. 17)**.

14 Make a stitch: 1xE, 1xB, 3xA. Pass through two more of the base ring beads. Make a stitch, and step up to exit the third tip bead of the stitch.

15 Repeat steps 4 **(fig. 18)** and 5.

16 Complete the motif by adding 2xA over the tip bead of the fourth stitch **(fig. 19)**.

Finishing
17 Repeat the link section.

18 Keep working, alternating the motif and link sections until the necklace is the length you like.

Finish each end of the necklace with two link sections and add a loop of beads over the end tip beads. This helps the necklace to lie neatly at the back of the neck. It also makes a base to attach simple jump rings and clasps **(fig. 20)**.

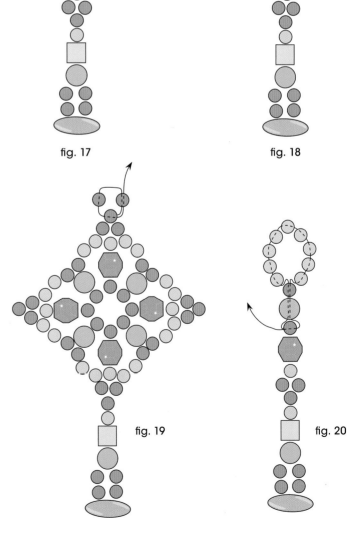

fig. 17

fig. 18

fig. 19

fig. 20

I'm happy to admit that this is among my favorites. It is so light and easy to wear, while making a "beady" statement. The beaded ribbon is easy to work and drapes well; use it for this design or add your own motifs. The lariat is worked in two directions: First make a motif section, and then work from the base row to make the ribbon section, which ends with a second motif section.

Deco Delight

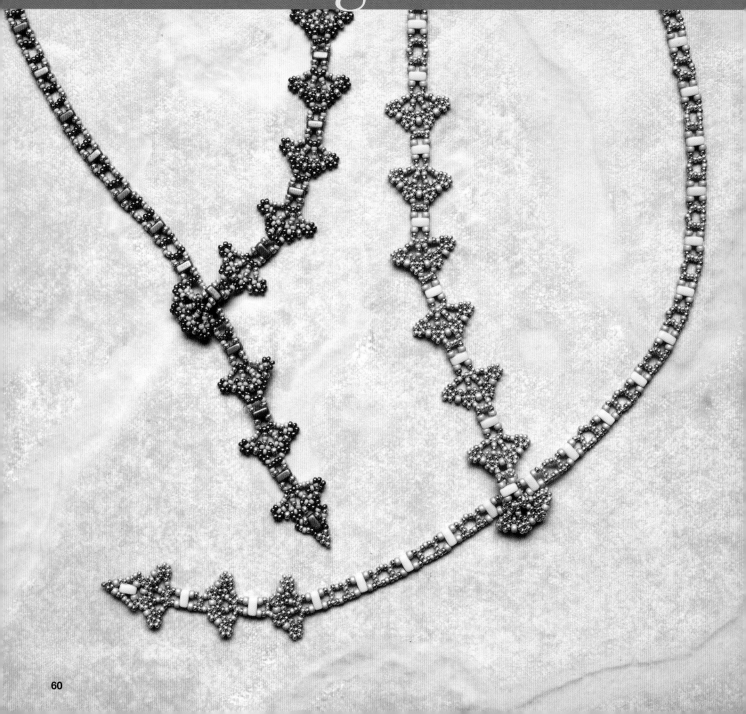

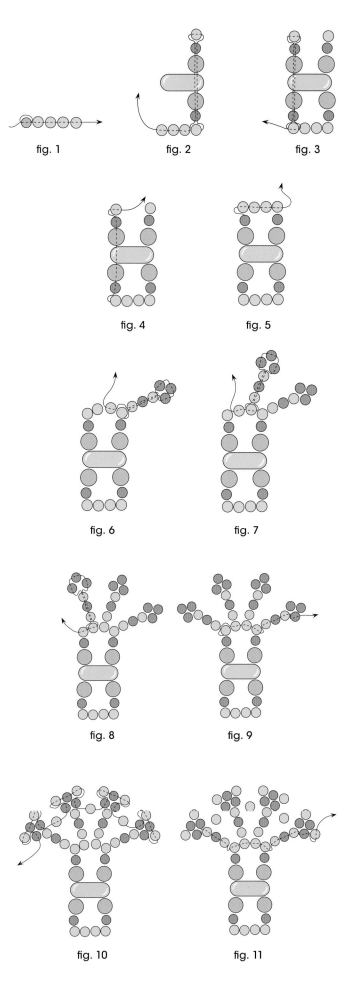

materials

11⁰ seed beads

- **A** 15g Duracoat zest
- **B** 15g Duracoat teal
- **C** 15g galvanized matte light green

D 10g 8⁰ seed beads, Duracoat matte light green

E 42 CzechMate two-hole brick beads, opaque pale turquoise

- 2 6mm jump rings
- Lobster clasp or similar

For a longer lariat, use 1xE for each link section.

1 Secure a stop bead. Pick up 4xA **(fig. 1)**, and push them down to the stop bead.

2 Make a stitch: 1xB, 1xD, 1xE, 1xD, 1xB (stalk); 1xA (tip). Pass back through the stalk beads and 3xA base row beads. Remove the stop bead and secure the tail to the working thread **(fig. 2)**.

3 Make a stitch: 1xB, 1xD. Pass through the second hole of the 1xE, 1xD, 1xB (stalk); 1xA (tip). Pass back through the stalk beads and the base row bead started from. Then pass back up through the stitch to exit the tip bead **(fig. 3** and **4)**.

4 Spacer Row: Pick up 2xA between the 1xA tip beads **(fig. 5)**.

Motif

5 Place a stitch over the first bead of the spacer row: 1xC, 1xB, 1xC (stalk); 3xB (tip). Pass back through the stalk beads and the next spacer bead **(fig. 6)**.

6 Place a stitch over the next bead of the spacer row: 1xC, 1xB, 1xC (stalk); 3xB (tip). Pass back through the stalk beads and the spacer bead started from, then pass through the next spacer bead **(fig. 7)**.

7 Repeat step 6 **(fig. 8)**.

8 Repeat step 6. After passing back through the stalk beads, pass through 3xA spacer row beads, the stalk beads, and the first tip bead of the first stitch **(fig. 9)**.

9 Spacer Row: Pick up 1xA between each tip bead of each stitch **(fig. 10)**.

fig. 1

fig. 2

fig. 3

fig. 4

fig. 5

fig. 6

fig. 7

fig. 8

fig. 9

fig. 10

fig. 11

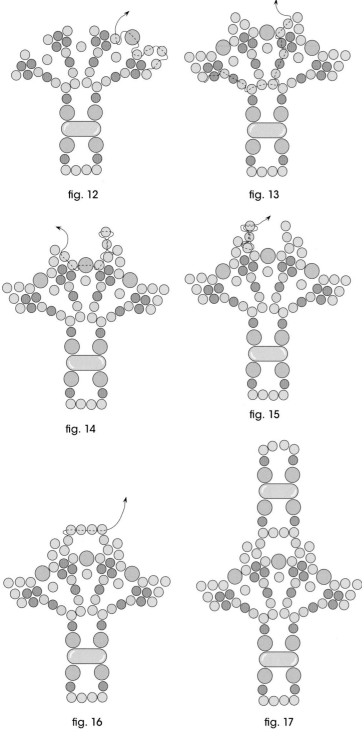

10 Weave back through the beads to exit the first bead added in step 9 **(fig. 11)**.

11 Pick up 3xA and pass through the next A bead added in step 9. Pick up 1xD and pass through the fourth A bead added in step nine **(fig. 12)**.

12 Repeat step 11 to add 3xA at the top of each stitch tip, and 1xD between each stitch. After adding the last 3xA, weave through the beads to exit the first of the 3xA added over the second stitch **(fig. 13)**. This completes the first motif.

Link Section

13 Add a stitch: 1xC (stalk); 1xA (tip) and pass back through the stalk. Weave through the beads to exit the first bead of the 3xA added over the third stitch **(fig. 14)**.

14 Add a stitch: 1xC (stalk); 1xA (tip), pass back through the stalk, the 1xA started from, and then step back up through the stitch to exit the 1xA tip bead **(fig. 15)**.

15 Spacer Row: Pick up 2xA between the 2xA tip beads **(fig. 16)**. Repeat steps 2–4 to make a link section **(fig. 17)**. Work a total of seven motifs separated with link sections, ending with a motif.

Double Motif

The end of the first section has a double motif, which creates a channel for the lariat to slide through.

1 Work from the spacer row at the base of the last link section (the one before the seventh motif). Work a link section and a motif. Add the first row of embellishment (1xA between tip beads) **(fig. 18)**.

2 Fold the two end motifs so they align. Pick up 1xA and pass through the center bead of the 3xA on the first motif. Pick up 1xA and pass through the next 1xA on the second motif. Pick up 1xD and pass through the 1xA on the second motif **(fig. 19)**.

fig. 12

fig. 13

fig. 14

fig. 15

fig. 16

fig. 17

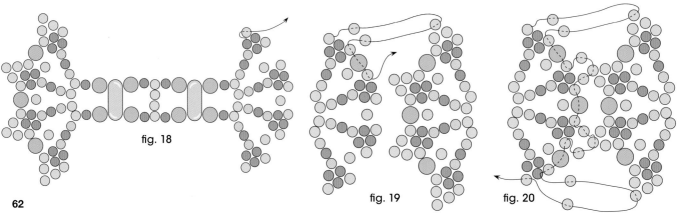

fig. 18

fig. 19

fig. 20

3 Repeat step 1 to continue joining the motif edges together through the center beads of the 3xA sets of the first motif **(fig. 20)**.

Ribbon

Return to the original base row and work a ribbon. The ribbon has alternate link sections and stitch sections. The necklace shown has a ribbon with 31 link sections, Start with a stitch section and end with a link section.

1 Make a stitch over the first and last bead of the spacer row: 1xB, 1xC, 1xB (stalk); 1xA (tip) **(fig. 21)**

2 Spacer Row: Pick up 2xA between the two 1xA tip beads **(fig. 22)**.

3 Work a link section: 1xB, 1xD, 1xE, 1xD, 1xB (stalk); 1xA (tip) **(fig. 23)**.

4 Spacer Row: Pick up 2xA between the two 1xA tip beads **(fig. 24)**.
   Repeat steps 1–4 to complete the ribbon **(fig. 25)**. Thread the end through the channel made at the opposite end of the work.

Second End

Work three motifs separated by link sections. End with a motif.

Embellish the End Motif

1 Weave through the beads to exit the center bead of the 3xA added over the second stitch of the final motif. Pick up 1XC, 1xD, 1xE, 1xD, 1xC, and pass through the center bead of the 3xA added over the third stitch of the final motif. Pass back through the beads just added to exit the tip bead started from in this step **(fig. 26)**.

2 Pick up 1xC, 1xB, 1xA, 1xB, 1xC. Pass through the second hole of the 1xE **(fig. 27)**.

3 Pick up 1xC, 1xB, 1xA, 1xB, 1xC. Pass through the 1xA started from in step one. Weave through the beads to exit the second hole of the 1xE **(fig. 28)**.

4 Pick up 1xA, 1xD, 4xB. Pass back through the first of the 4xB. Pick up 1xD, 1xA, and pass back through the second hole of the 1xE **(fig. 29)**. Finish the thread tails.

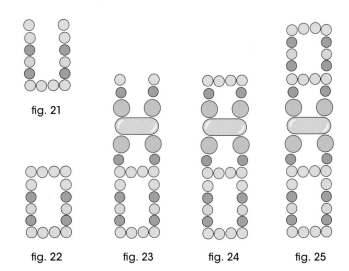

fig. 21

fig. 22   fig. 23   fig. 24   fig. 25

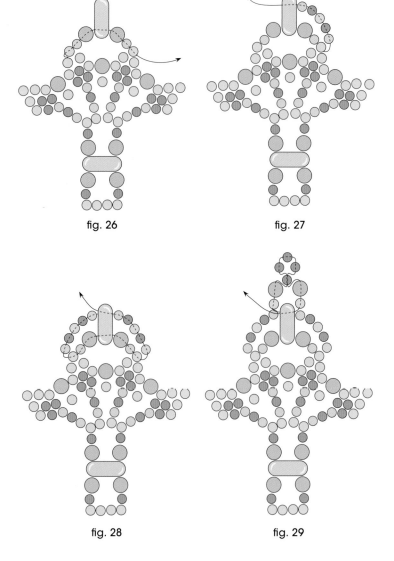

fig. 26   fig. 27

fig. 28   fig. 29

Vintage Lace uses the same ribbon and feather motifs, but in a different formation to create a dainty, yet substantial bracelet. The finished beadwork is rich in texture, just like the vintage cotton lace that first inspired the design. (Please note the diagrams show a shortened section with two completed motifs throughout.)

Vintage Lace

materials

11° seed beads

○ **A** 10g galvanized light lilac

● **B** 10g galvanized dusty orchid

○ **C** 10g matte pale mauve

● **D** 6g 8° seed beads, dusty orchid

▭ **E** 14 CzechMate two-hole bricks, opaque lilac luster

• Inline clasp or similar

note

The cream and copper colored bracelet replaces the brick beads with CzechMate two-hole tile beads. The tiles are deeper than the bricks, so the regular stitches have an extra seed bead at each end of the stalk. This design also works with half-Tila and Tila two-hole beads.

Bead Count

Here's how to determine the right number of beads for your measurements.

Each feather section has two brick bead stitches with one regular stitch in between, using 11 beads of the base row. Between each completed feather section is one regular stitch, using three base-row beads. The feather sections join above the middle bead of the three base-row beads. There is one additional base row at the start and end for the edge stitches.

For my bracelet of seven feather sections:
• Start and end: 2+2=4 beads
• Each section needs 11+3=14 beads and measures 2cm (¾ in.) 14x7=98
• Therefore, my start row is 4+98=102.
• To make the bracelet longer, just add 14 to the total for each additional 2cm required.

1 Secure a stop bead. Pick up 102 A beads (or your required number) and push them down to the stop bead **(fig. 1)**.

2 Make the first stitch over the end bead of the base row: 3xA (stalk); 1xA (tip). Pass through the next two beads of the base row **(fig. 2)**.

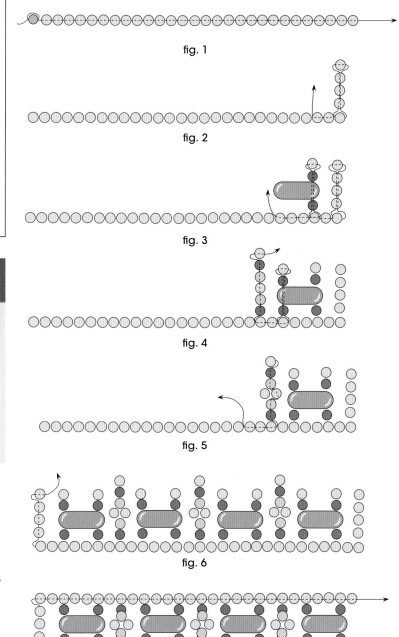

fig. 1

fig. 2

fig. 3

fig. 4

fig. 5

fig. 6

fig. 7

3 For the next stitch: Pick up 1xB, 1xE, 1xB (stalk); 1xA (tip). Pass back through the stalk, the bead on the base row, then pass through three more beads on the base row **(fig. 3)**.

4 For the next stitch: Pick up 1xB, pass through the second hole of the 1xE, 1xB (stalk); 1xA (tip). Pass back through the stalk beads, the bead on the base row, and through two more beads on the base row.

This completes the brick bead stitch. Note how it sits with two base beads between the stitches.

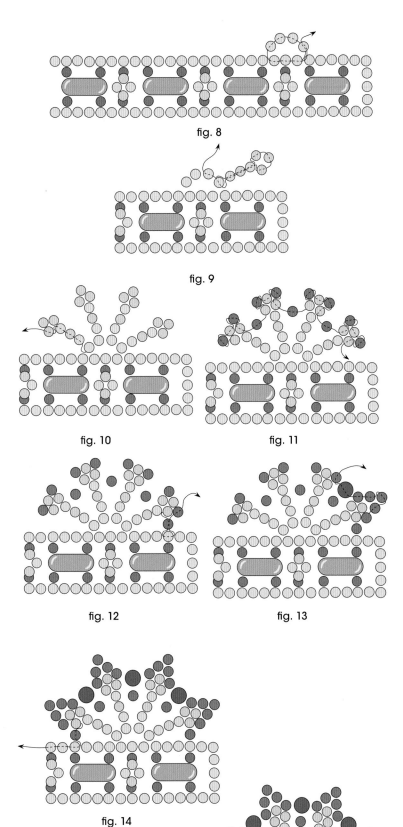

fig. 8

fig. 9

fig. 10

fig. 11

fig. 12

fig. 13

fig. 14

fig. 15

5 For the next stitch: Pick up 1xB, 1xC, 1xA, 1xC, 1xB (stalk); 1xA tip **(fig. 4)**. Pass back through 1xB and 1xC stalk beads, pick up 1xA, pass down through 1xC and 1xB stalk beads, and pass back through the base row bead. Pass through two base row beads **(fig. 4** and **5)**.

This completes the regular stitch. It is longer and will fold when the spacer row is added. Note how this stitch has one bead on either side of the base row.

6 Repeat steps 2–5 until all the brick bead stitches are in place. After the last brick bead stitch, you should have two base row beads remaining. Check that you have an even number of brick bead stitches—remember, a pair is needed for each completed feather.

7 Exit the end base row bead and remove the stop bead. Pick up 3xA (stalk); 1xA (tip). Pass back through the stalk beads and the end bead, then step up to exit the tip bead **(fig. 6)**.

8 Spacer Row: Pick up 1xA between the first and second tip beads, 2xA between the tip beads of the brick bead stitches, and 1xA between the other tips **(fig. 7)**. Pull the thread firmly to straighten the row, allowing the longer stitches to curve slightly. Weave down and back up the end stitch to secure the thread.

Feather Edge

1 Bring the needle through the spacer row to exit between the sixth and seventh bead from the end. *Pick up 4xA. Pass through the ninth, eighth, and seventh beads of the spacer row, and the first bead of the 4xA just added **(fig. 8)**.

2 Place a stitch over each bead of the 4xA: 1xA, 1xC, 1xA (stalk); 3xA (tip) **(fig. 9)**. After the fourth stitch, weave back through the beads to exit the first tip bead **(fig. 10)**.

3 Spacer Row: Pick up 1xB between each tip bead **(fig. 11)**.

4 Pick up 1xB and pass through the furthest tip bead of the brick bead stitch. Pass back through the 1xB and 1xA, and the 1xB of the first stitch tip **(fig. 12)**.

5 Pick up 3xB and pass through the next 1xB on the first stitch tip. **Pick up 1xD and pass through the first 1xB on the second stitch tip **(fig. 13)**.

6 Continue to place 3xB between the B beads on the stitch tips and 1xD between the stitches. At the end of the row, pass through the last 1xB and the 1xA stitch tip bead. Pick up 1xB, pass through the second tip bead on the spacer row of the next brick bead stitch. Pass through the spacer bead row to exit between the 7th and 8th bead from bead started from **(fig. 14)**.

7 You are now in place to add the next 4xA to start the next feather motif **(fig. 15)**. Work a feather motif, repeating the steps from the * of step 1 through step 4.

8 Pick up 1xB, pass through the center B of the 3xB over the last stitch of the previous motif. Pick up 1xB, pass through the next 1xB of the second motif. Continue from ** of step 5 **(fig. 16)**.

9 Keep working until you have completed all the feather motifs for one side of the bracelet **(fig. 17)**. Turn the bracelet over and repeat to add feather motifs along the second side. Check that the first one lines up with the first one on the original side **(fig. 18)**.

Center Embellishment

Fig. 19–21 show the center band of beadwork as outlines and the new beads in color to make it easier to see the thread paths.

1 Exit the spacer row between the sixth and seventh bead from the end. Pick up 2xC and pass through the nearest 1xC of the two C beads in the center of the regular stitch. Pick up 2xC, pass through the spacer bead before the tip bead, the tip bead of the regular stitch, and the spacer bead after it **(fig. 19)**.

2 Pick up 2xC and pass through the second 1xC of the two C beads in the middle of the regular stitch. Pick up 2xC and pass through the tip bead, two spacer beads, and tip bead of the next brick bead stitch **(fig. 20)**.

3 Continue along the center section, embellishing each regular stitch through the center C beads **(fig. 21)**.

note

I use Inline three-part clasps. Similar in design to watch clasps, they are dainty but very secure and ideal for bracelets. Simply sew the end bars to the end stitches of the bracelet.

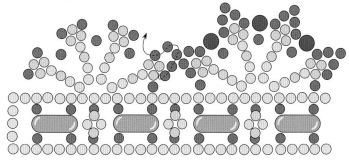

fig. 16

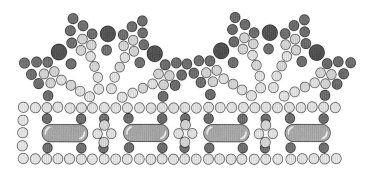

fig. 17

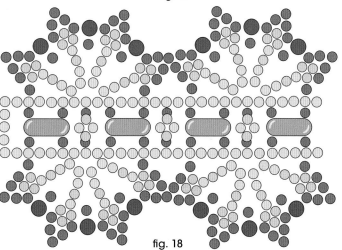

fig. 18

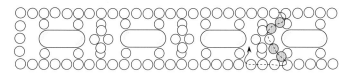

fig. 19

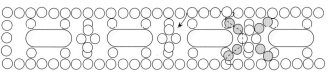

fig. 20

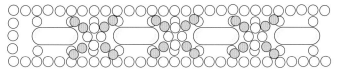

fig. 21

This pendant uses the feather motif around a beaded bezel for a 14mm rivoli, with sparkling bicone crystals nestling in the design. I love this as a simple pendant, but several can be stitched together through the edge beads to make bigger cuffs, too. For the pendant, a loop and an Albion stitch bail make it easy to string on any beaded cord, chain, or ribbon.

Noveley Lace

materials

15° seed beads
- ○ **A** 3g Duracoat zest
- ● **B** 3g Duracoat bright pink

11° seed beads
- ● **C** 6g Duracoat bright pink
- ○ **D** 6g matte opaque light pink

- ● **E** 4g 8° seed beads, Duracoat bright pink

- ⬡ **F** 4 4mm Swarovski bicone crystals, Padparadscha
- • 14mm Swarovski rivoli, Padparadscha

Miyuki seed beads are best for this design.

This Albion stitch bezel starts with a row of peyote stitch. Usually, a peyote stitch bezel pulls the beads up into a firm ring. Here, though, keep the tension softer and the beadwork just as flat as shown in the illustrations.

Bezel

1 Alternating C and D, pick up 32 beads and secure in a ring. Exit a D **(fig. 1)**.

2 Peyote stitch one round in C beads. The C beads will sit over the C beads of the base ring. The thread passes through the D beads and down to exit a bead on the inner edge of the ring **(fig. 2)**.

3 Place a stitch between each C bead of the inner edge: 2xA (stalk); 1xB (tip) **(fig. 3)**.

4 Step up to exit the tip bead of the first stitch. Then, pass through all the tip beads to draw them into a ring. Weave through the beads to exit a C bead on the outer edge of the bezel **(fig. 4)**. This forms the back of the bezel.

5 Place a stitch between the C beads of the outer ring: 1xD, 1xA (stalk); 1xB (tip) **(fig. 5)**. Step up to exit the tip bead of the first stitch.

6 Spacer Row: Pick up 1xB between each tip bead **(fig. 6)**.

7 Drop the rivoli into the bezel, face up. Pull the spacer row so it forms a neat ring, holding the rivoli in place. Weave through the beadwork to exit a C bead (middle row of peyote stitch) **(fig. 7)**.

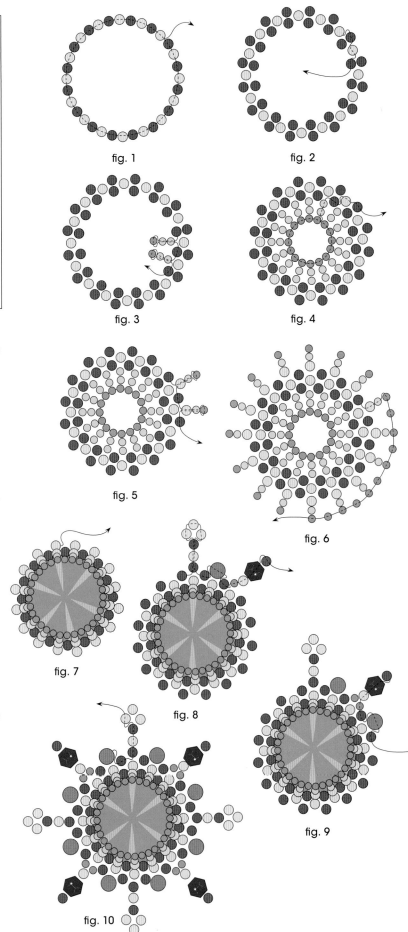

fig. 1

fig. 2

fig. 3

fig. 4

fig. 5

fig. 6

fig. 7

fig. 8

fig. 9

fig. 10

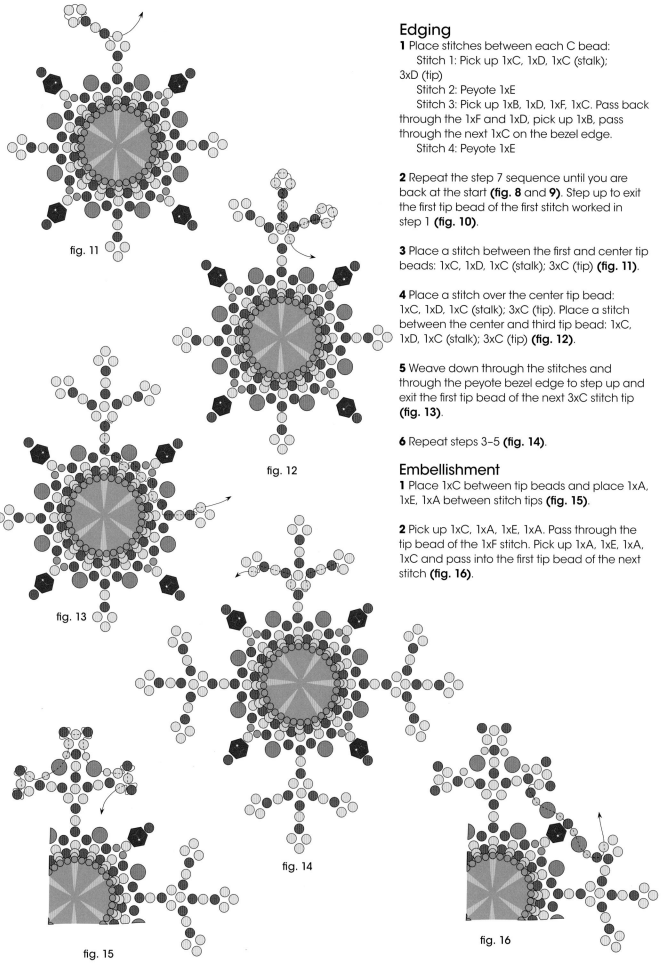

Edging

1 Place stitches between each C bead:
   Stitch 1: Pick up 1xC, 1xD, 1xC (stalk); 3xD (tip)
   Stitch 2: Peyote 1xE
   Stitch 3: Pick up 1xB, 1xD, 1xF, 1xC. Pass back through the 1xF and 1xD, pick up 1xB, pass through the next 1xC on the bezel edge.
   Stitch 4: Peyote 1xE

2 Repeat the step 7 sequence until you are back at the start **(fig. 8** and **9)**. Step up to exit the first tip bead of the first stitch worked in step 1 **(fig. 10)**.

3 Place a stitch between the first and center tip beads: 1xC, 1xD, 1xC (stalk); 3xC (tip) **(fig. 11)**.

4 Place a stitch over the center tip bead: 1xC, 1xD, 1xC (stalk); 3xC (tip). Place a stitch between the center and third tip bead: 1xC, 1xD, 1xC (stalk); 3xC (tip) **(fig. 12)**.

5 Weave down through the stitches and through the peyote bezel edge to step up and exit the first tip bead of the next 3xC stitch tip **(fig. 13)**.

6 Repeat steps 3–5 **(fig. 14)**.

Embellishment

1 Place 1xC between tip beads and place 1xA, 1xE, 1xA between stitch tips **(fig. 15)**.

2 Pick up 1xC, 1xA, 1xE, 1xA. Pass through the tip bead of the 1xF stitch. Pick up 1xA, 1xE, 1xA, 1xC and pass into the first tip bead of the next stitch **(fig. 16)**.

fig. 11

fig. 12

fig. 13

fig. 14

fig. 15

fig. 16

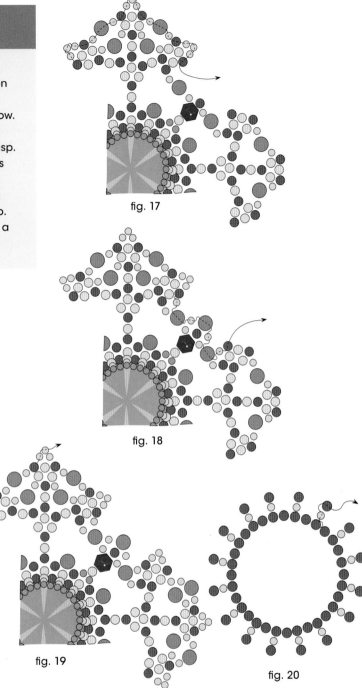

fig. 17

fig. 18

fig. 19

fig. 20

3 Repeat steps 1 and 2 until you are back at the start. Step up to exit the first 1xC added in step 1.

4 Place 3xA between the B beads at the stitch tips. Place 1xA, 1xE, 1xA between the stitch tips **(fig. 17)**.

5 Exit the 1xC, pick up 1xA, and pass through the 1xE added in step 2. Pick up 1xA, 1xE, 1xA, and pass into the next 1xE of step two. Pick up 1xA, pass into the first 1xC of the next stitch tip **(fig. 18)**.

6 Repeat steps 4 and 5 until you are back at the start. Step up to exit the center A bead of the 3xA above the center stitch of the first feather **(fig. 19)**.
   Leave the thread and set this piece aside.

The Bail
1 Pick up 32xC and secure in a ring.

2 Place a stitch over alternate beads of the ring: 1xA (stalk); 1xC (tip). At the end of the round, step up to exit a tip bead **(fig. 20)**.

3 Spacer Round: Pick up 1xC between each tip bead. Weave through the ring of beads a second time and then finish off the thread tails.

Add a Top Loop
At the top of the pendant, pick up 1xE, 1xD, 1xA, 15xD, 1xA. Pass the needle and thread through the bail. Pass back down through 1xD and 1xE. Weave through all these beads a second time to make a nice, secure loop. Finish off the thread tails **(fig. 21)**.

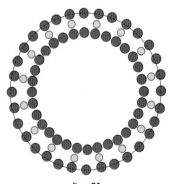

fig. 21

Sometimes, all you need is a delicate necklace. Dainty Days is a design that is quick and easy to work up. The scale is also perfect for younger bead fans. Like the previous designs, this makes full use of the multi-tip stitch to create pretty feathery shapes.

Dainty Days

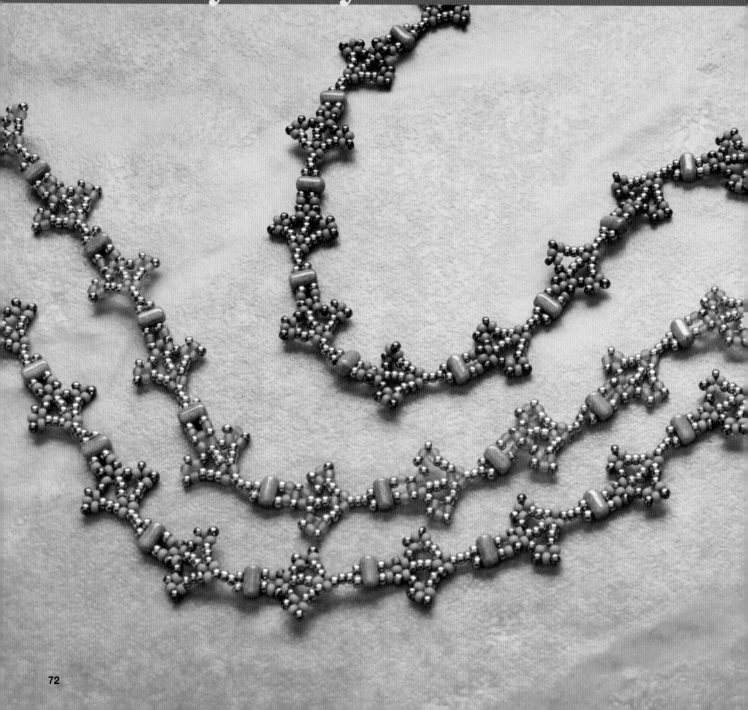

materials

11⁰ seed beads

○ **A** 10g Duracoat light orchid

● **B** 10g Duracoat bright pink

● **C** 10g matte frosted turquoise

▬ **D** 20 Czech two-hole Rulla beads, opaque turquoise

• 2 6mm jump rings

• Lobster claw clasp

Motif

1 Secure a stop bead. Pick up 1xA, 1xC, 1xA, and push them down to the stop bead **(fig. 1)**.

2 Stitch 1: Pick up 1xC, 1xD (stalk); 1xA (tip). Pass back through the stalk beads through 1xC, 1xA of the base row. Remove the stop bead and secure the tail to the working thread **(fig. 2)**.

3 Stitch 2: Pick up 1xC, pass through the second hole of the 1xD (stalk); 1xA (tip). Pass back through the 1xD, 1xC and the 1xA base row bead. Step up to exit the tip bead **(fig. 3 and 4)**.

4 Stitch 3: Pick up 3xA (stalk); 3xC (tip). Pass back through the stalk beads, then through the tip bead of the stitch worked in step 1 **(fig. 5)**. Pass through the beads of the first stitch, the base row, and the beads of the second stitch. Then step up through the stitch just worked to exit the first 1xC tip bead **(fig. 6)**.

5. Place a stitch between tip beads: 3xA (stalk); 3xC (tip) **(fig. 7)**.

6 Place a stitch over the center tip bead: 3xA (stalk); 3xC (tip) **(fig. 8)**.

7 Place a stitch between tip beads: 3xA (stalk); 3xC (tip). Weave through the beads to exit the first tip bead of the stitch added in step 5 **(fig. 9)**.

8 Pick up 1xB, pass through the center tip bead of the first stitch. Pick up 1xB, pass through the third tip bead of the first stitch **(fig. 10)**.

9 Pick up 1xB, pass through the first tip bead of the second stitch. Pick up 1xB, pass through the second tip bead of the second stitch. Pick up 1xB, pass through the third tip bead of the second stitch **(fig. 11)**.

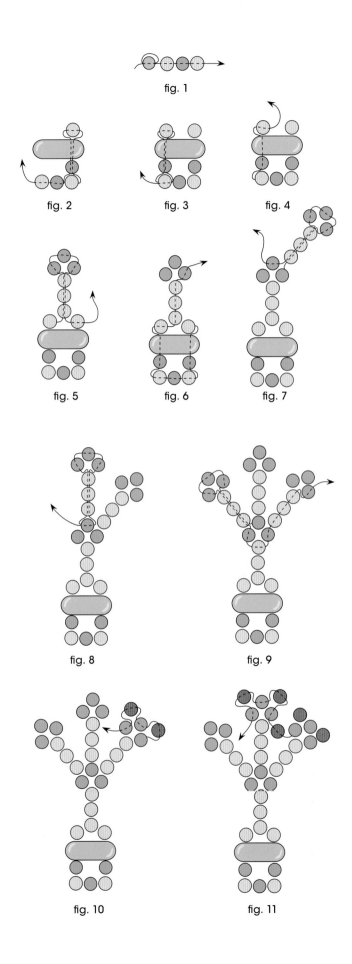

fig. 1

fig. 2

fig. 3

fig. 4

fig. 5

fig. 6

fig. 7

fig. 8

fig. 9

fig. 10

fig. 11

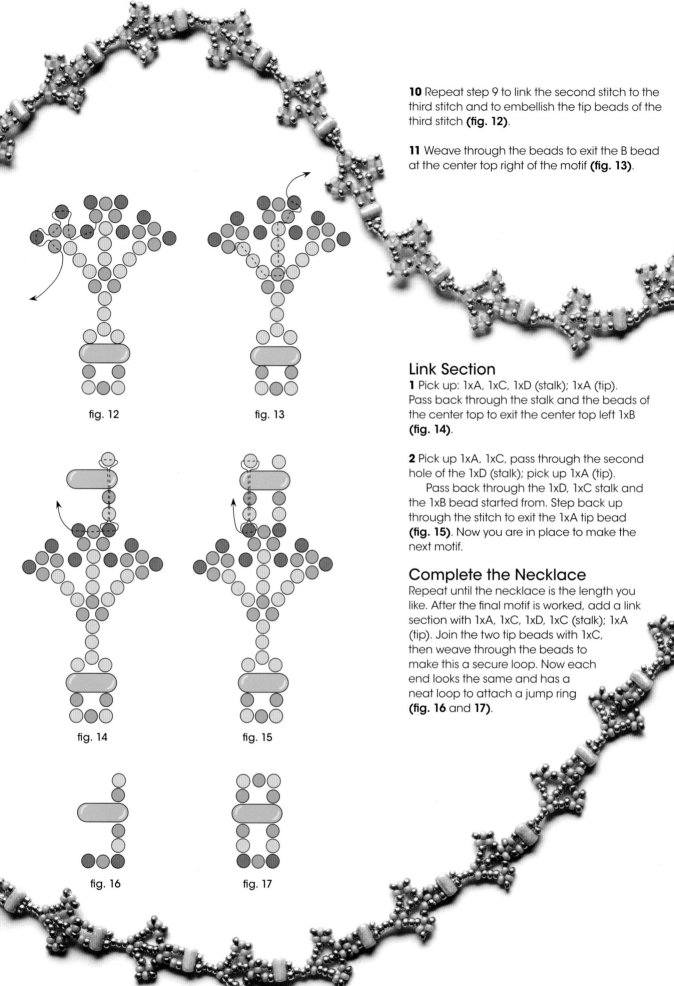

10 Repeat step 9 to link the second stitch to the third stitch and to embellish the tip beads of the third stitch **(fig. 12)**.

11 Weave through the beads to exit the B bead at the center top right of the motif **(fig. 13)**.

fig. 12

fig. 13

Link Section

1 Pick up: 1xA, 1xC, 1xD (stalk); 1xA (tip). Pass back through the stalk and the beads of the center top to exit the center top left 1xB **(fig. 14)**.

2 Pick up 1xA, 1xC, pass through the second hole of the 1xD (stalk); pick up 1xA (tip).
Pass back through the 1xD, 1xC stalk and the 1xB bead started from. Step back up through the stitch to exit the 1xA tip bead **(fig. 15)**. Now you are in place to make the next motif.

Complete the Necklace

Repeat until the necklace is the length you like. After the final motif is worked, add a link section with 1xA, 1xC, 1xD, 1xC (stalk); 1xA (tip). Join the two tip beads with 1xC, then weave through the beads to make this a secure loop. Now each end looks the same and has a neat loop to attach a jump ring **(fig. 16** and **17)**.

fig. 14

fig. 15

fig. 16

fig. 17

Structure and Links

With little snippets from the previous chapters, I will now show you how to create designs that bring them together in different ways. These projects are more detailed and introduce the ways in which I use Albion stitch to build structures— raising stitches from the surfaces and edges of the basic flat or tubular stitch.

COLOR INSPIRATION

This is one of the easiest color palettes to play around with, a neutral blend inspired by well-worn leather, vintage metal, sun-bleached linen, and dusty burlap. They are popular because they are familiar and easy to wear. This sophisticated blend of neutrals are kept lively by mixing in bead finishes with a luster coating along side matte or color-lined translucent beads along side more robust metallic and solid colors.

The heart of these circles is the basic bezel from the Noveley Lace pendant. The edges are embellished with more stitches and the circles are linked together with variations of the basic Albion stitch ribbon. (These instructions are for the necklace on the right.)

Roundelay Ribbon

materials

15º seed beads
○ **A** 6g matte antique silver Duracoat

◐ **B** 6g light gray luster

11º seed beads
○ **C** 10g matte antique silver Duracoat

◐ **D** 10g color-lined transparent gold

● **E** 10g metallic dark bronze

 F 22 CzechMate two-hole brick beads, light green Picasso

 G 11 CzechMate two-hole tile beads, brown Picasso

• 2 jump rings
• Lobster claw clasp

Motif

1 Pick up 32xC beads and secure in a ring. Exit a C bead **(fig. 1)**.

2 Peyote stitch one round in D beads. Step down and exit a bead on the inner edge of the ring **(fig. 2)**.

3 Place a stitch between each C bead of the inner edge: 2xB (stalk); 1xA (tip) **(fig. 3)**.

4 Step up to exit the tip bead of the first stitch, then pass through all the tip beads to draw them into a ring. Weave through the beads to exit a D bead on the outer edge **(fig. 4)**.

5 Place a stitch between the D beads of the outer ring: 2xB, 1xE (stalk); 1xB (tip). Pass back through 1xE, 1xB, pick up 1xB, and pass through the next D bead of the outer ring **(fig. 5)**.
   Repeat until you are back at the start and step up to exit the tip bead of the first stitch **(fig. 6)**.

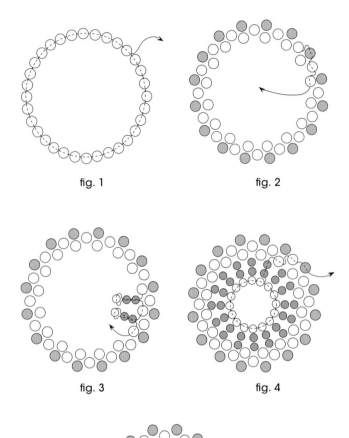

fig. 1 fig. 2

fig. 3 fig. 4

fig. 5

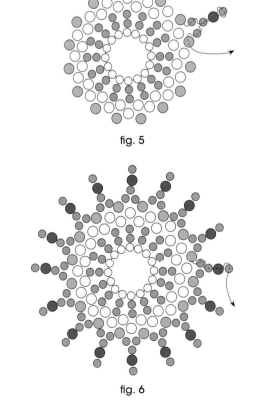

fig. 6

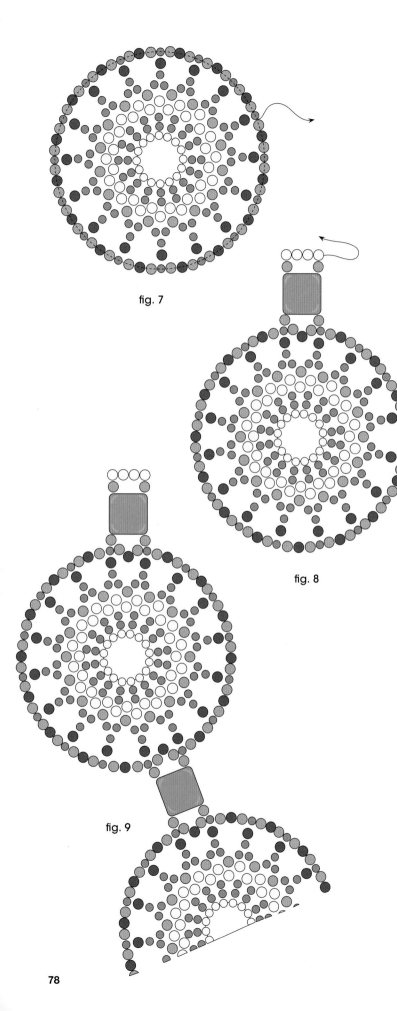

fig. 7

fig. 8

fig. 9

6 Spacer Row: Place 1xD, 1xE, 1xD between each tip bead. Finish off the thread tails and set this piece aside **(fig. 7)**.

7 Make a total of four motifs.

Joining the Motifs

1 Exit a B tip bead on a motif edge. Make a stitch: 1xD, 1xG, 1xD (stalk); 1xC tip. Pass back through the stalk beads and the 1xB, then pass through the beads to exit the next 1xB tip bead. Pick up 1xD, pass through the second hole of the 1xG, then pick up 1xD (stalk) and 1xC (tip). Weave back through the stalk beads (1xD, 1xG, 1xD). Step up and place 2xC between the tip beads. This will form the base of the ribbon for one side of the necklace **(fig. 8)**.

2 Weave through the edge beads to exit the eighth B tip bead from the stitch just worked. Pick up 1xD, 1xG, 1xD, and pass through a 1xB tip bead on the edge of a second motif. Pass back through the beads, the starting 1xB, and through to exit the ninth B on the first motif edge. Pick up 1xD, pass through the second hole of the 1xG, pick up 1xD, and pass through the next 1xB on the second motif edge. Pull the thread up to secure this link **(fig. 9)**. Join the remaining motifs together in the same way.

Necklace Ribbon

1 To start the necklace ribbon, which will be attached to the last motif, weave through to exit the third B tip bead to the right of the link joining this motif to the previous one. Pick up 1xD, 1xF, 1xD, 1xF, 1xD (stalk); 1xC (tip). Pass back through the stalk beads, the starting B, and then on through the edge beads to exit the next B tip bead.

2 Pick up 1xD, pass through the second hole of the F. Pick up 1xD, pass through the second hole of the next F, pick up 1xD, and 1xC (tip). Pass back through the stalk beads, then the starting B. Step up to exit the C tip bead **(fig. 10)**.

3 Spacer Row: Pick up 2xC between the tip beads. Now you are in place to work a ribbon of alternating sections.
   Section 1: Make stitches with F beads
   Section 2: Place two stitches each with 2xD, 1xC, 1xE, 1xC, 2xD (stalk); 2xA (tip)
   Section 3: Pick up 1xD, 1xG, 1xD (stalk); 1xC (tip). Repeat the sequence **(fig. 11)** until the necklace is the length you require.

Go back to the spacer row of the section worked at the top of the first motif and work the ribbon as before.

Attach a clasp of your choice to the ribbon ends.

The ribbon elements can be joined at any point on a circle edge. The designs shown use asymmetry to create the basic necklace shape. Make several motifs and lay them out in different ways until you find a layout that works for you.

Smaller or larger motifs are made in the same way; just change the number of beads in the start ring. For smaller motifs, shorten the inner stitches to 1xB (stalk); 1xB (tip). For larger motifs, you may need to add B beads to both the inner and outer stitches.

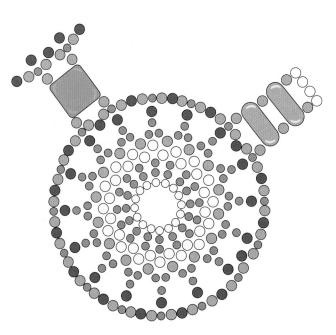

fig. 10

note

The motifs can be worked to either match or be designed in a medley of colors, with each motif delivering a different combination.

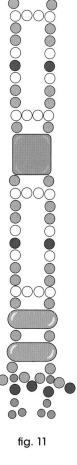

fig. 11

Maderon Arches are built from the surface of a band of flat Albion stitch. Each rib of this articulated cuff has two half-moon sides, which are laced across the top with Rizo accent beads to add a spiky edging. The base is embellished for more texture. It takes time, but results in a wonderfully sturdy statement piece.

Maderon Arches

materials

 A 6g 15º seed beads, metallic silver

11º seed beads

○ **B** 15g metallic silver

○ **C** 5g color-lined transparent green

⬭ **D** 112 Rizo beads, transparent olive AB

• 3-strand sliding clasp or similar

The bracelets shown measure 17cm (7 in.), not including clasp. Each arch uses 7xD. Each arch section measures 1cm (½ in.), including the embellished row.

note

It is possible to work the flat ribbon base first and then add the arch sections, but having tried it several ways, I prefer to work as described in the instructions: building one section at a time. You can simply work until the bracelet is the right length. The grid base has one block of grid at each end, one for each arch, and one between each arch.

fig. 1

1 Secure a stop bead. Pick up 10xB and push them down to the stop bead **(fig. 1)**.

2 Place a stitch over the first, fourth, seventh and tenth bead of the base row: 2xB (stalk); 1xB (tip). Step up through the beads of the last stitch to exit the tip bead **(fig. 2)**.

fig. 2

3 Spacer Row: Pick up 2xB between each tip bead **(fig. 3)**.

4 Repeat steps 2 and 3 two more times. This will give you a grid of three rows of stitches with nine apertures between them **(fig. 4)**.

5 Embellish the first row of stitches: Exit a tip bead and pick up 1xA, 1xC, 1xA. Pass through the two beads between stitches on the base row **(fig. 5)**.

Pick up 1xA and pass through the 1xC just added. Pick up 1xA and pass through the next tip bead of the grid **(fig. 6 and 7)**.

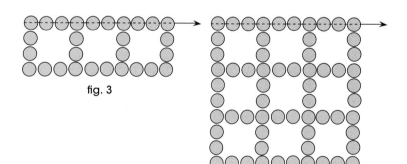

fig. 3   fig. 4

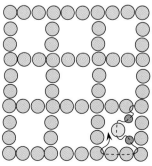

fig. 5

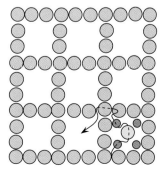

fig. 6

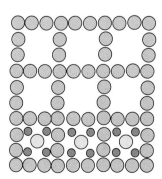

fig. 7

6 Exit the center left tip of the first row of stitches. Pick up 5xB, pass through the center right tip bead of the first row of stitches, and then through 1xB of the 5xB just added **(fig. 8)**.

7 Place a stitch over each bead of the 5xB: 1xC (stalk); 1xB (tip) **(fig. 9)**. Weave through the beads of the base to exit the tip bead of the end stitch **(fig. 10)**.

8 Spacer Row: Pick up 1xB between each tip bead **(fig. 11)**.

9 Pass through the beads to the center left tip bead of the next row of stitches on the base **(fig. 12)**.

10 Repeat steps 7–9. At the end of the spacer row (step 9), pass through the end tip bead of the base row and back through 2xB of the spacer row **(fig. 13)**.

Now there are two arch sections, which need to be joined together. The diagrams show an overhead view **(fig. 14)**.

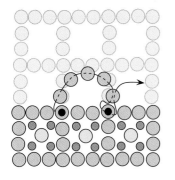
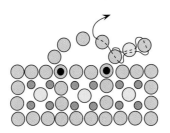

fig. 8   fig. 9

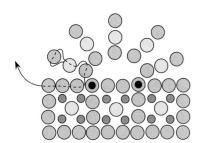
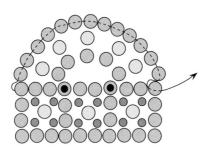

fig. 10   fig. 11

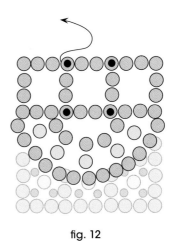

fig. 12

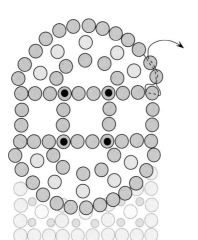

fig. 13

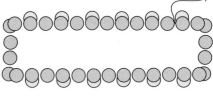

fig. 14

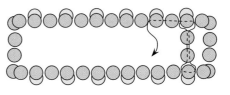

fig. 15

11 Pick up 2xB, pass through the first tip bead of the first arch section and back through the 2xB. Pass back through the tip bead started from and through two more beads of the second arch spacer row (to exit the next tip bead) **(fig. 15)**.

12 Repeat step 11 to link the tip beads of the arches. At the end of the row, exit the end bead of the base row **(fig. 16)**.

Now the first arch is completed and ready for embellishment.

13 Pick up 1xA, 1xD, 1xA and pass through the first spacer bead of the first arch.

14 Pick up 1xA, pass through the 1xD, pick up 1xA, and pass through the first tip bead of the second arch. Repeat to embellish each aperture of the arch **(fig. 17)**.

15 Embellish the last row of the base grid, just as you did the first row (step 5). The first section is now complete.

To work the following sections, first add two rows of base stitches. Add two arches over the base beads (as marked in **fig. 18** with black dots), then embellish the next row of stitches.

Once the piece is the right length, work one more row of base stitches and embellish it as before. This will give you matching ends to the bracelet. Stitch the sliding clasp to the end rows of beads.

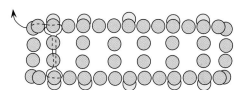

fig. 16

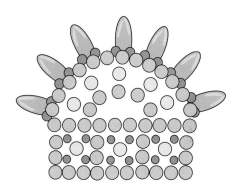

fig. 17

fig. 18

For this design, we return to the circle and build a donut of stitches. I've made these in many combinations and love their sturdiness. The edges can be laced just like the Maderon arches, with any combination of accent beads, including one- and two-hole beads.

Retro Rings

materials

- ○ **A** 6g 15º seed beads, antique pewter metallic

- ● **B** 10g 11º seed beads, antique pewter metallic

- ⬭ **C** 36 SuperDuo two-hole beads

- ⬡ **D** 48 3mm fire-polished beads

- ○ **E** 10g 8º seed beads, antique pewter metallic

- Strips of jersey cotton fabric (notes, p. 87)
- 2 jump rings
- Lobster claw clasp

The larger retro rings use 12xC each and the smaller ones use 12xD. The necklace shown has three large and four small rings.

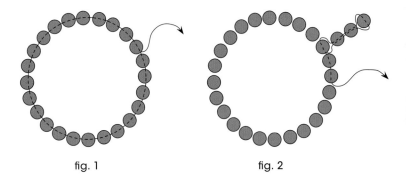

fig. 1   fig. 2

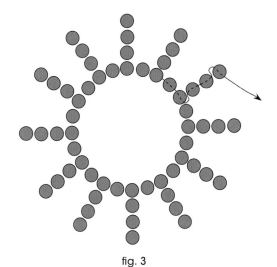

fig. 3

Small Retro Ring

1 Pick up 24xB; secure them in a ring **(fig. 1)**.

2 Place a stitch over alternate beads of the base ring: 2xB (stalk); 1xB (tip)**(fig. 2)**. Step up to exit the tip bead of the first stitch **(fig. 3)**.

3 Spacer Round: Pick up 1xB between each tip bead **(fig. 4)**. You now have a little tube one stitch high **(fig. 5)**.

4 Add the embellishment: Exit a tip bead, pick up 2xA, 1xD, 2xA, and pass through the spacer bead on the base ring **(fig. 6)**.

5 Pick up 1xA and pass through 1xA, 1xD, 1xA. Pick up 1xA and pass through the next tip bead on the spacer round **(fig. 7, 8** and **9)**.

Large Retro Ring

1 Pick up 24xB and secure them in a ring **(fig. 1)**.

2 Place a stitch over alternate beads of the base ring: 2xB (stalk); 1xB (tip) **(fig. 2)**. Step up to exit the tip bead of the first stitch **(fig. 3)**.

3 Spacer Round: Pick up 1xB between each tip bead **(fig. 4)**. You now have a little tube one stitch high. This forms the inner ring of the donut shape **(fig. 5)**.

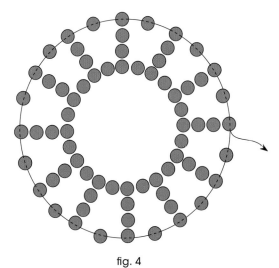

fig. 4

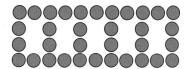

fig. 5

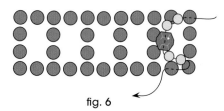

fig. 6

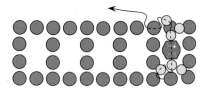

fig. 7

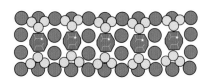

fig. 8

fig. 9

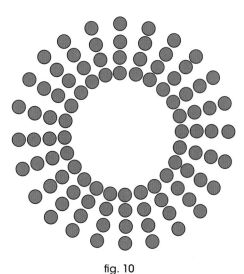

fig. 10

4 Place a stitch over every bead of the spacer round: 2xB (stalk); 1xB tip **(fig. 10)**.

5 Spacer Round: Pick up alternate 1xA and 1xC between the tip beads **(fig. 11)**.

6 Weave through to exit a bead on the base round and repeat step 4 **(fig. 10)**.

7 Exit a tip bead and check the alignment to add the spacer bead round. Use the second hole of the 1xC and place 1xB alternately **(fig. 12)**.

8 Weave through the beads to exit a 1xB spacer bead. Pick up 1xE and pass through the opposite 1xB spacer bead. Pass back through the 1xE, then on through the edge beads to exit the next 1xB spacer bead **(fig. 13)**. Repeat until you are back at the start and then finish off the thread tails **(fig. 14)**.

Beaded Endcap

Make the start ring to fit snug over your chosen necklace base. Use an even number of beads to make the ring.

1 Pick up 24 (or your chosen number) xB and secure them in a ring **(fig. 1)**.

2 Place a stitch over alternate beads of the base ring: 2xB (stalk); 1xB (tip) **(fig. 2)**. Step up to exit the tip bead of the first stitch **(fig. 3)**.

3 Spacer Round: Pick up 1xB between each tip bead **(fig. 4)**.

4 Repeat steps 2 and 3.

5 Repeat step 2, then step up to exit a tip bead and pass through all the tip beads to draw them into a ring.

6 Stitch 1xE across the ring of beads just as you did for the embellishment of a large ring.

Next, pick up 9xA and secure them over the ring of beads. This will form a loop to hold the jump rings for the clasp **(fig. 15)**.

7 Bring the ends of the cotton strips together and stitch them into the end cap, passing through the beads and through the fabric until secure.

8 Embellish the first row of stitches of the end cap in the same way as the small rings were embellished, but substitute 1xD with 1xE. Thread the retro rings onto the fabric strips, then repeat the steps to add a second end cap.

fig. 11

notes

- The silver sample uses SuperDuo, CzechMate triangle, and Preciosa Pip beads as accent beads on the larger rings. The smaller rings have either 3mm crystals or two O beads with an 11º seed bead between them.

- I've used strips of fabric cut from "retired" T-shirts; it's a fun way to create a yarn. Lay a T-shirt flat and cut off the hem, then cut 2.5cm (1-in.) slices from the bottom of the body section. Stretch each slice and the edges will roll to form a rolled ribbon. I like this soft ribbon and it's fun to find T-shirts in the colors you need. Bring several colors together to complement your beading colors. Keen crafters can dye white T-shirt strips for one-of-a-kind ribbons.

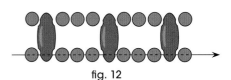

fig. 12

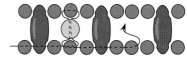

fig. 13

fig. 14

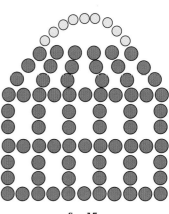

fig. 15

Tubular Albion stitch lies at the heart of these lovely links, Swarovski rose montées add a vintage sparkle and a new twist on using a two-holed accent. Combined with Retro Rings Luxe links give you all sorts of design options from a deluxe pendant to a lavish chain. Simple embellishment adds lots of texture to the surfaces.

Luxe Links

materials

- **A** 5g 15º seed beads, metallic silver

11º seed beads
- **B** 5g metallic silver
- **C** 10g color-lined transparent honey

- **D** 3g 1.8mm cube beads, metallic pewter
- **E** 4g 8º seed beads, color-lined light olive green
- **F** 13 4mm Swarovski rose montées, crystal AB

1 Pick up 16xC and secure them in a ring **(fig. 1)**.

2 Place a stitch over alternate beads of the base ring: 1xC (stalk); 1xC (tip). Step up to exit the tip of the last stitch worked **(fig. 2)**.

3 Spacer Round: Pick up 1xC between each 1xC tip bead **(fig. 3)**.

4 Place a stitch over each tip bead of the previous round: 1xC, 1xE, 1xD, 1xC (stalk); 1xC (tip). Step up to exit a tip bead **(fig. 4)**.

5 Spacer Round: Pick up 3xC between each tip bead, exit a tip bead when the round is secure **(fig. 5)**.

6 Place a stitch over each tip bead and each center bead of the 3xC: 1xC (stalk); 1xC (tip) **(fig. 6)**.

7 Spacer Round: Pick up 1xC between each 1xC tip bead, exit a tip bead **(fig. 7)**.

8 For this round, place a stitch over each tip bead of the previous round, but stitches will share Fs: 1xC, 1xF, 1xC (stalk); 1xC (tip). Pass back through the stalk beads, the tip bead started from, and through to exit the next tip bead of the base round **(fig. 8)**.
　Pick up 1xC, pass through the second channel of the 1xF, pick up 1xC (stalk); 1xC (tip). Pass back through the 1xC, 1xF (facing outwards),

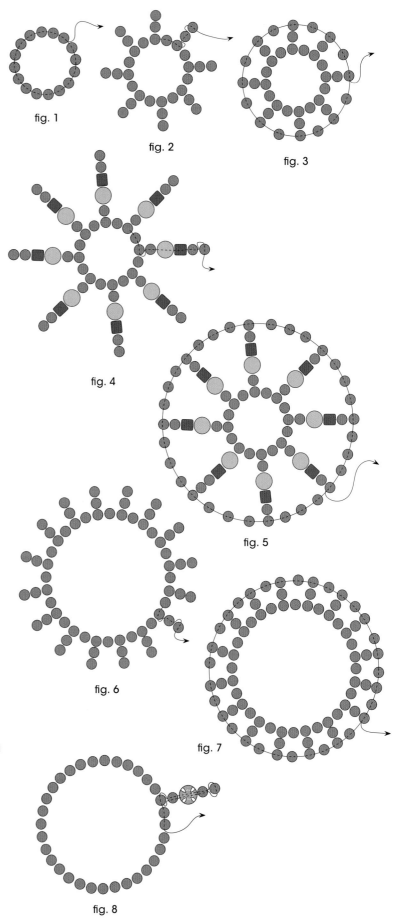

fig. 1

fig. 2

fig. 3

fig. 4

fig. 5

fig. 6

fig. 7

fig. 8

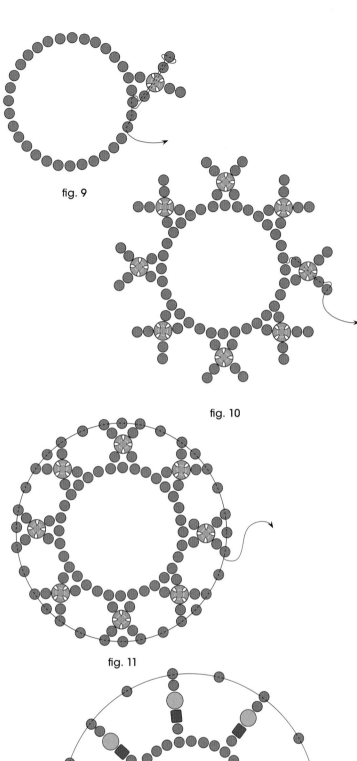

fig. 9

fig. 10

fig. 11

fig. 12

1xC, and pass through the base round bead started from **(fig. 9)**.

Repeat all the way around, then step up to exit a tip bead **(fig. 10)**.

9 Spacer Round: Pick up 1xC between each tip bead **(fig. 11)**.

10 Place a stitch over every fourth bead of the spacer round: 1xC, 1xD, 1xE, 1xC (stalk); 1xC (tip).

11 Spacer Round: Pick up 1xC between each tip bead. Exit a tip bead once the round is secure **(fig. 12)**.

12 Repeat step 2. Add a spacer round of 1xC between each tip bead **(fig. 3)**. The base is now completed.

Bail

1 Exit a bead on the spacer round (it is easier to see if this is a tip bead). Pick up 19xC and pass through the sixth bead from the one started from. Pass back through the last 2xC added **(fig. 13)**.

2 Place a stitch over alternate beads of the new loop: 1xC (stalk); 1xC (tip). At the end of the row, pass through to exit the tip bead next to the one started from in step one **(fig. 14)**.

3 Spacer Round: Pick up 1xC between each tip bead. Exit the last tip bead, pick up 1xC, and pass through the next tip bead on the base ring **(fig. 15)**.

Add a bail to the other end of the pendant in the same way. Check that you start in a position so that it will lie in the same orientation as the first loop.

Embellishments

Embellishments for the bail is added in the same way as for previous projects, crossing over the apertures. See pages 34 and 81 for further illustrations.

Bail Embellishment

First stitch: Pick up 3xA, return stitch 1xA, pass through center A of 3xA of first stitch, pick up 1xA **(fig. 16)**.

The top, two middle, and the bottom round of the pendant are embellished with this sequence: First stitch: Pick up 1xA, 1xB, 1xA. Return stitch: Pick up 1xA, pass through 1xC, pick up 1xA **(fig. 17)**.

Center Band Embellishment

1 Bring the needle out of 1xC stalk above a 1xF. Pick up 1xC, 1xD, 1xC, and pass through the 1xC stalk below the same 1xF. Pass through the spacer bead of the round below, then pass up through the next 1xC stalk bead **(fig. 18)**.

2 Pick up 1xC, pass through the 1xD of step one, pick up 1xC, and pass through the 1xC above the second 1xF. Pass through the spacer bead of the row above and the next 1xC stalk bead **(fig. 19)**.

Repeat to embellish each space between the Fs **(fig. 20)**.

Adding the Rings

The pendant has two rings: a larger one worked through the top bail and a smaller one worked through the bottom bail. Both are then embellished. It may feel fiddly at first, but it is quite easy to rotate the beading while it is on the bail as you work.

Larger Ring

1 Pick up 32xC, pass the thread through the bail at one end of the pendant, then secure the beads in a ring.

2 Place a stitch over alternate beads of the ring: 1xC (tip). Step up to exit a tip bead.

3 Spacer Round: Pick up 1xC between each tip bead.

4 Embellish the ring in the same way as the smaller retro ring is embellished (p. 86). Exit a tip bead, pick up 2xA, 1xC, 2xA. Pass through the spacer bead on the second edge of the ring. Pick up 1xA, pass through 1xA, 1xC, 1xA, pick up 1xA, pass through the next tip bead on the original edge of the ring. Repeat all the way around **(fig. 23)**.

Smaller Ring

1 Pick up 20xC, pass the thread through the second loop of the pendant, then secure the beads into a ring.

2 Place a stitch over alternate beads of the ring: 1xC (stalk); 1xC (tip). At the end of the round, step up to exit a tip bead.

3 Spacer Round: Pick up 1xC between each tip bead.

4 The embellishment on this ring alternates: Exit a tip bead, pick up 1xF, then pass through the space bead of the second edge in reverse direction. Pass through the second channel of the 1xF and through the next tip bead on the first edge of the ring **(fig. 21)**.

Embellish the next aperture: First stitch: 1xA, 1xC, 1xA, second pass 1xA, pass through the 1xC, pick up 1xA, and pass through the next tip bead.

Alternate these two embellishments until you are back at the start, and then finish off the thread tails **(fig. 22)**.

notes

- I used hollow mesh chain (you can also use SilverSilk), and beaded an end cap. Make a ring of an even number of beads to just fit around your cord or chain. Work stitches over alternate beads of the ring. Join the tips with single beads. Bead a loop across the end, and stitch the end cap to your cord or chain.

- The second color sample uses a mix of silver, gold, and bronze together with the same crystal AB montees and matte dark brown 8° seed beads.

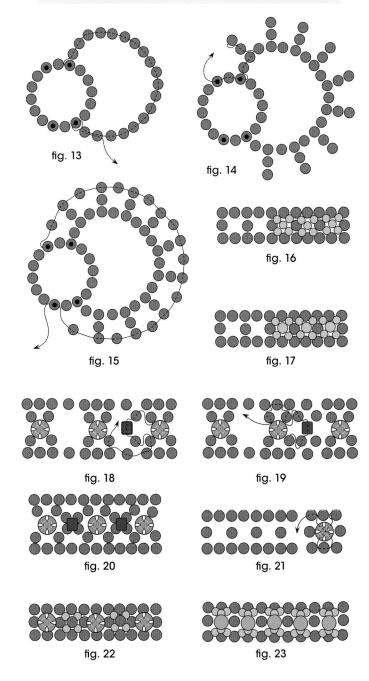

fig. 13

fig. 14

fig. 15

fig. 16

fig. 17

fig. 18

fig. 19

fig. 20

fig. 21

fig. 22

fig. 23

Layers of stitches are joined together to make a cube
and then nestling inside each section is an accent bead.
The dainty cubes can be strung together on bracelets and
necklaces or used as accent beads within other designs.

Nice Dice

materials

COLORWAY 1

 A 4g 11º seed beads, metallic plum

 B 5g 3mm bugle beads, transparent luster gold

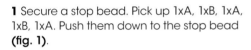 **C** 28 5mm fire-polished beads, topaz AB

- Chain necklace

COLORWAY 2

A 4g 11º seed beads, Duracoat pale pink
B 5g 3mm bugle beads, transparent luster violet
C 36 5mm fire-polished beads, violet AB

1 Secure a stop bead. Pick up 1xA, 1xB, 1xA, 1xB, 1xA. Push them down to the stop bead **(fig. 1)**.

2 Place a stitch over each A bead of the base row: 1xB (stalk); 1xA (tip) **(fig. 2)**. Remove the stop bead and secure the working thread to the tail, then step up to exit the tip of the last stitch worked **(fig. 3)**.

3 Spacer Row: Pick up 1xB between each tip bead **(fig. 4)**.

4 Repeat steps 2 and 3 **(fig. 5)**. Now you have a base grid of two rows of stitches with four apertures.

5 Place a stitch over each 1xA of the base grid: 1xB (stalk); 1xA (tip) **(fig. 6)**. Step up to exit the last stitch tip **(fig. 7)**.

note

Each cube uses seven fire-polished beads. These beads give a metallic sheen to colored beads, so it is a nice way to soften the starkness of this metallic theme. Choose solid colors for a more graphic looking dice.

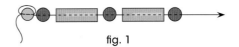

fig. 1

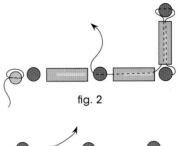

fig. 2

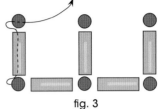

fig. 3

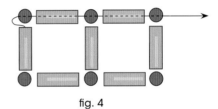

fig. 4

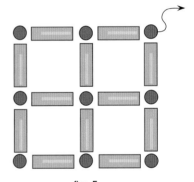

fig. 5

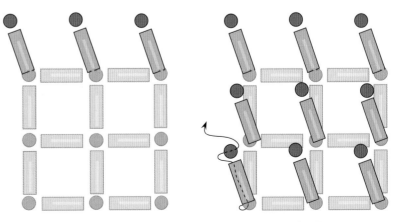

fig. 6   fig. 7

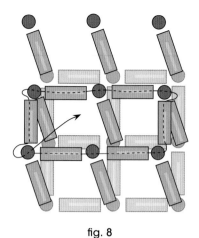

fig. 8

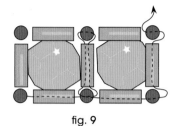

fig. 9

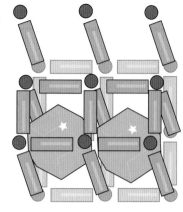

fig. 10

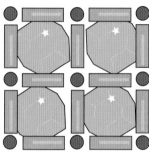

fig. 11

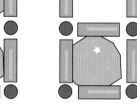

fig. 12

6 Spacer Row: Pick up 1xB between each tip bead of the first and second row of new stitches **(fig. 8)**.

7 Bring the needle through to exit the center 1xA tip of the first row of stitches. Drop 2xC into the beadwork and settle them so they sit inside the "box". Place 1xB between the bead started from and the center 1xA tip of the second row of stitches.

Weave through the beads to exit the end 1xA tip bead of the second row of stitches **(fig. 9** and **10)**.

8 Place 1xB between each of the remaining tip beads, then repeat step 7 **(fig. 11)**. This completes the first layer of the cube.

9 Repeat steps 5–8, but omit one 5mm crystal **(fig. 12)**.

The aperture without a crystal in it leaves space for the cube to be threaded on to cord or ribbon. If you plan to stitch the cubes together in a different way, fill the final aperture as before.

notes

- The length of bugle bead will determine the overall size of the finished cube. If you are worried about bugle beads cutting the thread, choose a named brand and choose from the matte or coated ranges—these are much less likely to have sharp edges.

- To make bigger cubes, increase the number of stitches in the start row, but remember, for each extra stitch, you will add a whole layer in order to keep a cube shape.

- I've used delicate ready-made ball chain and link chain. If adding findings to ribbons, cords, and chains isn't appealing, there are lots of ready-made options. All you need to do is check that the clasp findings attached to the chain are fine enough to pass through the beaded beads.

Conclusion

Thank you for joining me. It has been a pure pleasure to revisit Albion stitch and create all these new designs for you to explore. My fingers are already itching to make more, and perhaps that is what I love most about this stitch—it has endless possibilities. All you need is a willingness to pick out some beads and start to play. All of the designs in this book can be adapted to accommodate variations, and if you do experiment, please feel free to get in touch and show me your creations.

If you have enjoyed the projects in this book, you are welcome to join me in cyberspace. Follow my blog at *heather-beads.blogspot.co.uk* where I share my class listings and news of my beading life, or visit my website, *heatherworks.co.uk* for kits and patterns.

There is also a website just for Albion stitch, which is steadily growing to include a gallery of readers work, links to more patterns, and updates on new publications: *albionstitch.com.*

Acknowledgments

A beading book starts with an idea and ends with a beautiful, freshly printed book. In between are many months of work. My first thank you is to himself, who patiently keeps our boat afloat and remembers to cook supper, while I am immersed in beads.

My next is to Mary Wohlgemuth, who first commissioned this book, for the gift of believing in my ideas and to Karin Van Voorhees for the reassuring presence that is a really good editor. The Kalmbach team who helped make my ideas *look amazing* is Lisa Schroeder, Lisa Bergman, and Bill Zuback.

Each book is the work of many hands, the editor, photographers, designers, proofreaders, and ending with the guys who wrap the pallets of books as they roll off the press, and the ones who drive the vans to deliver them. Each person invests great care and knowledge into their part of the process. So to everyone involved, thank you so much for helping to make this little book into a big reality.

A special thank you is also due to my many students all over the world. You keep it real, share the laughter, and keep me focused on this amazing craft we share.

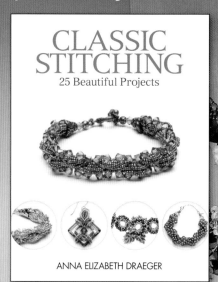